Additional Practice Workbook

GRADE K TOPICS 1–14

enVision® Mathematics

SAVVAS
LEARNING COMPANY

ISBN-13: 978-0-13-495374-8
ISBN-10: 0-13-495374-6

4 20

Grade K Topics 1–14

Topic 1
Numbers 0 to 5

Lesson 1-1 1
Lesson 1-2 3
Lesson 1-3 5
Lesson 1-4 7
Lesson 1-5 9
Lesson 1-6 11
Lesson 1-7 13
Lesson 1-8 15
Lesson 1-9 17
Lesson 1-10 19

Topic 2
Compare Numbers 0 to 5

Lesson 2-1 21
Lesson 2-2 23
Lesson 2-3 25
Lesson 2-4 27
Lesson 2-5 29

Topic 3
Numbers 6 to 10

Lesson 3-1 31
Lesson 3-2 33
Lesson 3-3 35
Lesson 3-4 37
Lesson 3-5 39
Lesson 3-6 41
Lesson 3-7 43
Lesson 3-8 45

Topic 4
Compare Numbers 0 to 10

Lesson 4-1 47
Lesson 4-2 49
Lesson 4-3 51
Lesson 4-4 53
Lesson 4-5 55

Topic 5
Classify and Count Data

Lesson 5-1 57
Lesson 5-2 59
Lesson 5-3 61
Lesson 5-4 63

Topic 6
Understand Addition

Lesson 6-1 65
Lesson 6-2 67
Lesson 6-3 69
Lesson 6-4 71
Lesson 6-5 73
Lesson 6-6 75
Lesson 6-7 77
Lesson 6-8 79

Topic 7
Understand Subtraction

Lesson 7-1 81
Lesson 7-2 83
Lesson 7-3 85
Lesson 7-4 87
Lesson 7-5 89
Lesson 7-6 91
Lesson 7-7 93

Topic 8
More Addition and Subtraction

Lesson 8-1 95
Lesson 8-2 97
Lesson 8-3 99
Lesson 8-4 101
Lesson 8-5 103
Lesson 8-6 105
Lesson 8-7 107
Lesson 8-8 109
Lesson 8-9 111
Lesson 8-10 113

Topic 9
Count Numbers to 20

Lesson 9-1 115
Lesson 9-2 117
Lesson 9-3 119
Lesson 9-4 121
Lesson 9-5 123
Lesson 9-6 125
Lesson 9-7 127

Topic 10
Compose and Decompose Numbers 11 to 19

Lesson 10-1 129
Lesson 10-2 131
Lesson 10-3 133
Lesson 10-4 135
Lesson 10-5 137
Lesson 10-6 139
Lesson 10-7 141

Topic 11
Count Numbers to 100

Lesson 11-1 143
Lesson 11-2 145
Lesson 11-3 147
Lesson 11-4 149
Lesson 11-5 151

Topic 12
Identify and Describe Shapes

Lesson 12-1 153
Lesson 12-2 155
Lesson 12-3 157
Lesson 12-4 159
Lesson 12-5 161
Lesson 12-6 163
Lesson 12-7 165

Topic 13
Analyze, Compare, and Create Shapes

Lesson 13-1 167
Lesson 13-2 169
Lesson 13-3 171
Lesson 13-4 173
Lesson 13-5 175
Lesson 13-6 177
Lesson 13-7 179

Topic 14
Describe and Compare Measurable Attributes

Lesson 14-1 181
Lesson 14-2 183
Lesson 14-3 185
Lesson 14-4 187
Lesson 14-5 189
Lesson 14-6 191

Name _____

Another Look!

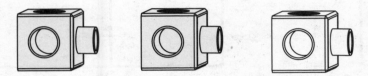

HOME ACTIVITY Have your child count groups of 1, 2, and 3 objects.

 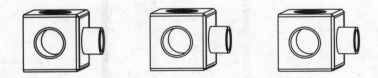

 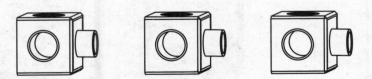

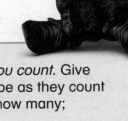

Directions Say: *Use connecting cubes or other objects to model making 2, and then color a cube for each cube you count.* Give students 3 cubes or other small counting objects. Have students: ⭐ choose 2 cubes or objects, and then color a cube as they count each cube to show how many; ❷ choose 1 cube or object, and then color a cube as they count each cube to show how many; ❸ choose 3 cubes or objects, and then color a cube as they count each cube to show how many.

4

5

6

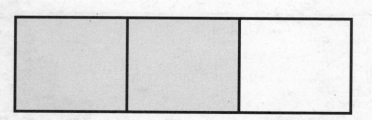

7

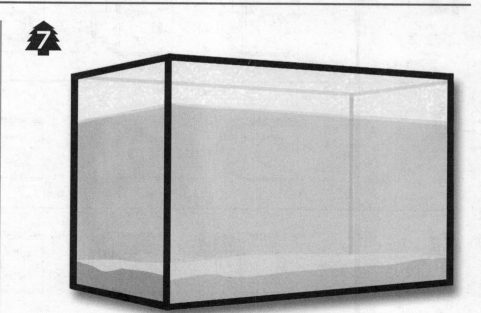

Directions **4** and **5** Have students color a box as they count each animal to show how many. **6 Higher Order Thinking** Have students draw a bird as they count each colored box that shows how many. **7 Higher Order Thinking** Have students draw 1 plant, 2 fish, and 3 rocks in the tank.

Name _____

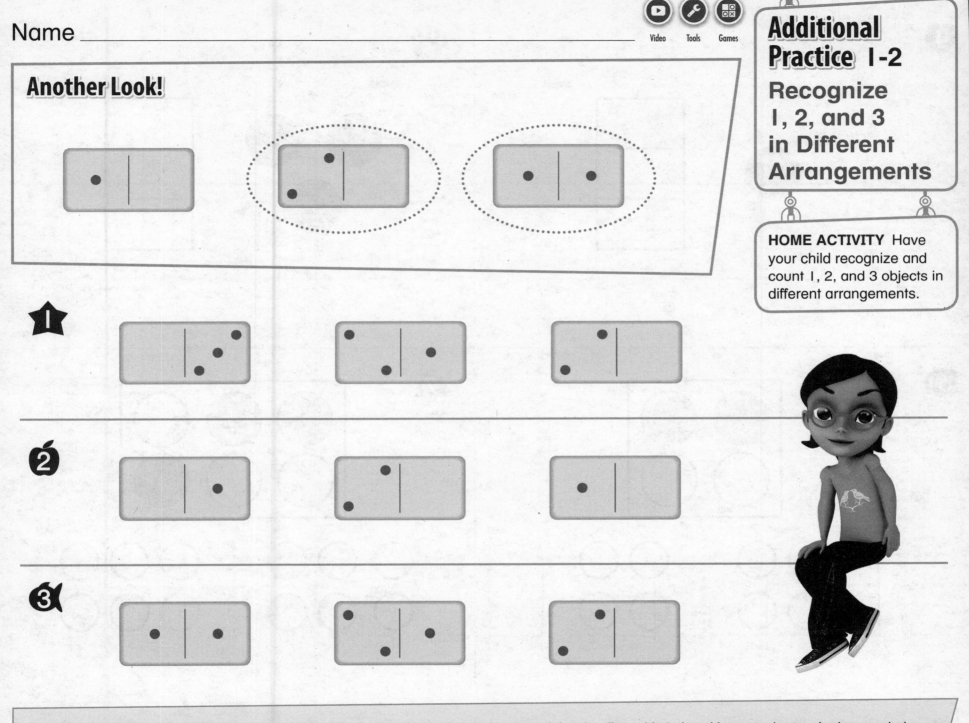

Additional Practice 1-2

Recognize 1, 2, and 3 in Different Arrangements

HOME ACTIVITY Have your child recognize and count 1, 2, and 3 objects in different arrangements.

Another Look!

⭐ 1

🍎 2

🐟 3

Directions Say: *Count the dots on each dot tile, and then draw a circle around the dot tiles with 2 dots.* Have students: ⭐ draw a circle around the dot tiles with 3 dots; 🍎 draw a circle around the dot tiles with 1 dot; 🐟 draw a circle around the dot tiles with 2 dots.

4

5

6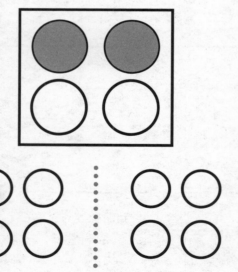

7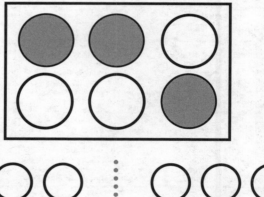

Directions **4** and ✋ Have students count the counters, and then color the boxes to show how many. **6** and 🌲 **Higher Order Thinking** Have students count the number of gray counters in the box, and then color the same number of counters in two different ways.

Name _____

Additional Practice 1-3
Read, Make, and Write 1, 2, and 3

Another Look!

 1 1 2 2 3 3

HOME ACTIVITY Draw groups of 1, 2, and 3 circles on 3 index cards. Have your child write the correct number on the back of each card. Then use the cards to practice counting and reading the numbers 1, 2, and 3.

❶

❷

_____

_ _ _ _ _ _ _ _ _ _ _ _

Directions Say: *Practice writing the numbers 1, 2, and 3.* Then have students: ❶ count the moons, and then write the number of moons under each picture; ❷ count the stars, and then write the number of stars under each picture.

3

_____

- - - - - - - - - - - -

_____

4

_____

- - - - - - - - - - - -

_____

5

_____

- - - - - - - - - - - -

_____

6

2

_____

- - - - - - - - - - - -

_____

7

6 six

Topic 1 | Lesson 3

Name _____

Another Look!

HOME ACTIVITY Have your child count groups of 4 objects. Then have him or her draw pictures of 4 objects. Repeat using the number 5.

⭐ 1

🍎 2

🐟 3

Directions Say: *Count the dots in the box. Draw a counter for each dot you count.* ⭐–🐟 Have students draw a counter for each dot they count.

Directions ❹ and ✋ Have students color a box as they count each flower to show how many. ☕ **Higher Order Thinking** Have students color red each group of 4 objects the clowns have and color yellow each group of 5 objects the clowns have. 🌲 **Higher Order Thinking** Have students draw 4 or 5 flowers, and then color a box as they draw each flower to show how many.

 Topic 1 | Lesson 4

Name _____

Another Look!

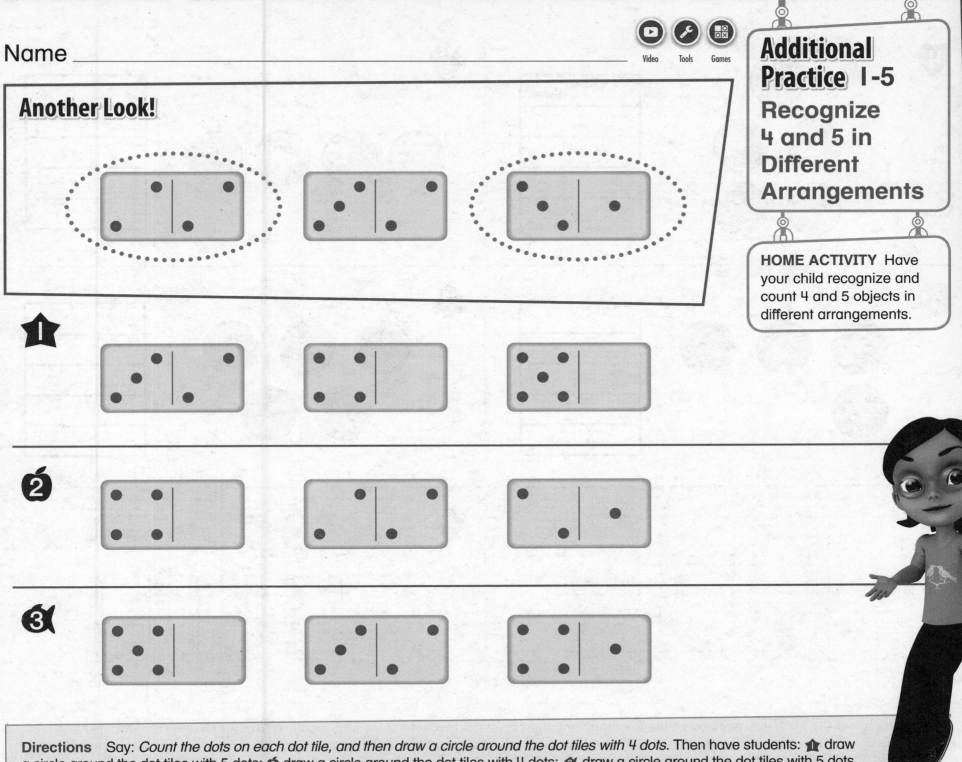

HOME ACTIVITY Have your child recognize and count 4 and 5 objects in different arrangements.

Directions Say: *Count the dots on each dot tile, and then draw a circle around the dot tiles with 4 dots.* Then have students: ⭐ draw a circle around the dot tiles with 5 dots; ❷ draw a circle around the dot tiles with 4 dots; ❸ draw a circle around the dot tiles with 5 dots.

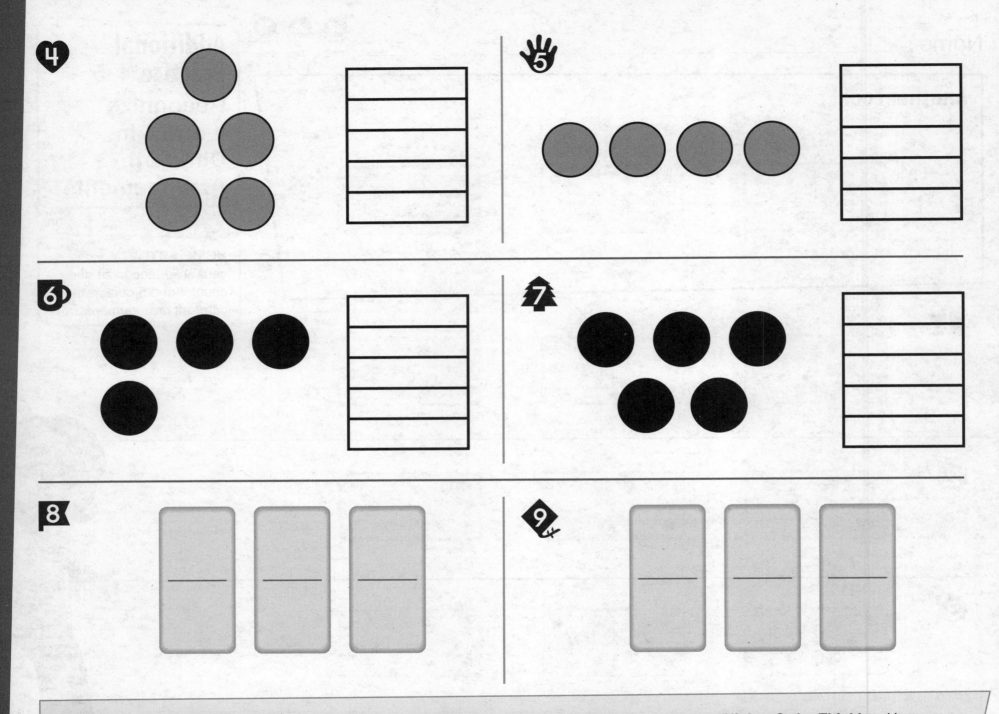

Directions 4–7 Have students count the counters, and then color the boxes to show how many. 8 **Higher Order Thinking** Have students draw 4 dots on each dot tile to show three different arrangements of dots. 9 **Higher Order Thinking** Have students draw 5 dots on each dot tile to show three different arrangements of dots.

Topic 1 | Lesson 5

Name _____

Additional Practice 1-6
Read, Make, and Write 4 and 5

Another Look!

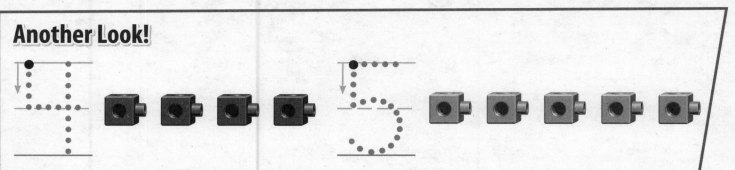

HOME ACTIVITY Draw groups of 4 and 5 circles on 2 index cards. Have your child write the correct number on the back of each card. Then use the cards to practice counting and reading the numbers 4 and 5.

⭐1 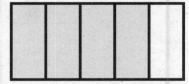 _____

🍎2 _____

⭐3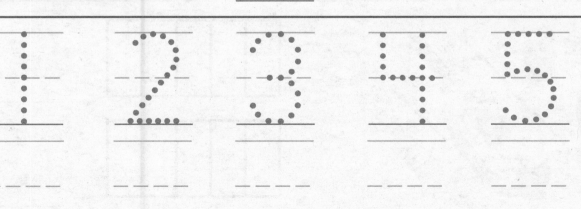

Directions Say: *Count the cubes, and then write the numbers to tell how many.* Have students: ⭐ and 🍎 count the colored boxes, and then write the number to tell how many; ⭐ write each number from 1 to 5, and then write each number again.

Directions ♥ and ✋ Have students count the number of birds, and then practice writing the number that tells how many. ☕ **Higher Order Thinking** Have students look at the number, and then draw counters to show how many. 🌲 **Higher Order Thinking** Have students count the bottles of paint and the tubes of paint, color a box for each and then write the numbers to tell how many.

Topic 1 | Lesson 6

Name _____

Another Look!

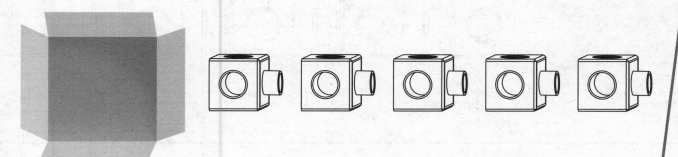

HOME ACTIVITY
Alternate putting objects on a plate and leaving it empty. Have your child identify when there are 0 objects on the plate.

1

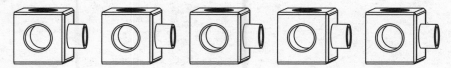

2

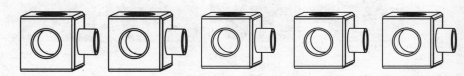

3

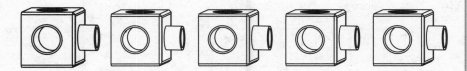

4

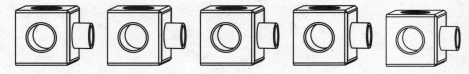

Directions Say: *How many toys are in the box? Use cubes or other objects to show 0, and then color 0 cubes.* Give students 5 cubes or 5 other objects. Have students: ★ choose 0 cubes or objects, and then color a cube as they count each cube to show how many; ❷ choose 2 cubes or objects, and then color a cube as they count each cube to show how many; ❸ choose 1 cube or object, and then color a cube as they count each cube to show how many; ❹ choose 4 cubes or objects, and then color a cube as they count each cube to show how many.

Name _____

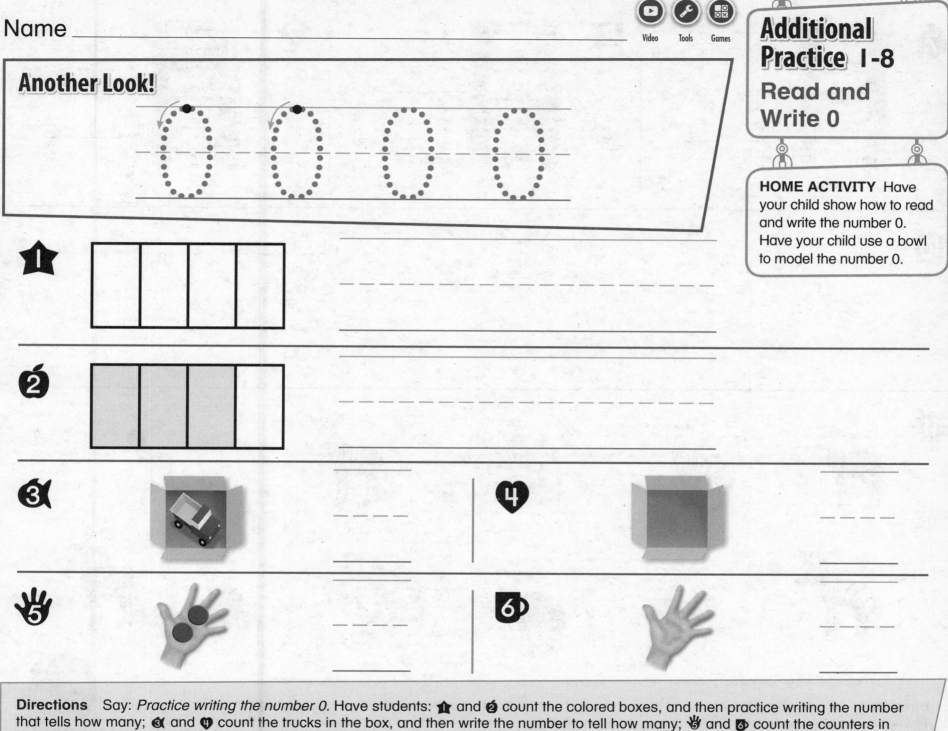

Another Look!

HOME ACTIVITY Have your child show how to read and write the number 0. Have your child use a bowl to model the number 0.

⭐1

2

3

4

5

6

Directions Say: *Practice writing the number 0.* Have students: ⭐ and 2 count the colored boxes, and then practice writing the number that tells how many; 3 and 4 count the trucks in the box, and then write the number to tell how many; 5 and 6 count the counters in the hand, and then write the number to tell how many.

7 ___ ___ ___

8 ___ ___ ___

9 ___ ___ ___

10 ___ ___ ___

Name _____

Another Look!

 1

 2

Directions Say: *The first row has zero counters colored. Write the number to tell how many. The next row shows 1 more counter colored. Write the number to tell how many.* ★ and ② Have students color counters to add 1 more counter to each row than the row before, and then write the number to tell how many.

3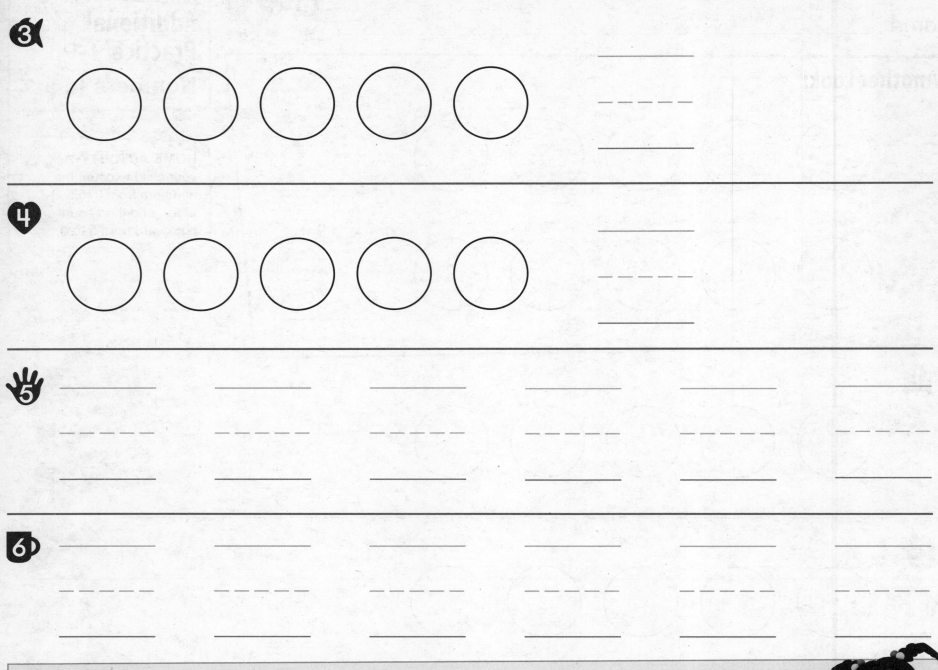

○ ○ ○ ○ ○

_ _ _ _ _

4

○ ○ ○ ○ ○

_ _ _ _ _

5

6

18 eighteen

Topic I | **Lesson 9**

Name _____

Additional Practice 1-10
Construct Arguments

Another Look!

1 chipmunk

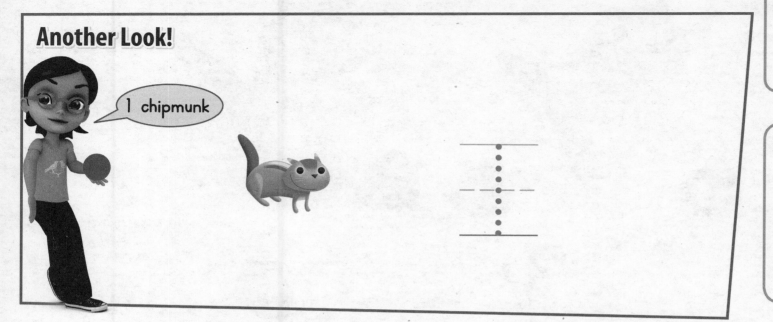

⭐

②

③

Directions Say: *Marta places 1 counter on the chipmunk and argues that there is 1 chipmunk. Practice writing the number to tell how many.* ⭐–③ Have students make a math argument about how many chipmunks are in each row, and then write the number. Have them use objects, words, or a method of their choice to explain their arguments and tell why they are correct.

Directions Read the problem to students. Then have them use multiple problem-solving methods to solve the problem. Say: *Some squirrels go out to gather acorns. How many squirrels and how many acorns are there?* ❹ **Make Sense** *What are you asked to find?* ✋ **Be Precise** *How many squirrels and how many acorns are there? Count the number of squirrels and the number of acorns, and then write the numbers to tell how many.* ❻ **Explain** *Make a math argument about how many squirrels and acorns there are. Use objects, words, or a method of your choice to explain your arguments and tell why you are correct.*

20 twenty

Name _____

Another Look!

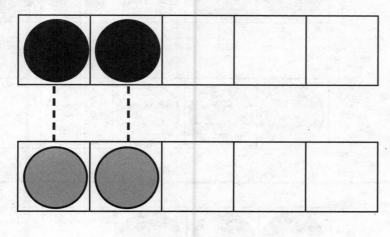

HOME ACTIVITY Give your child 5 objects. Place up to 5 objects on the table. Ask your child to make a group of objects that is equal in number to the group you made. Repeat with different numbers of objects. (Object suggestions: forks/spoons; pencils/pens)

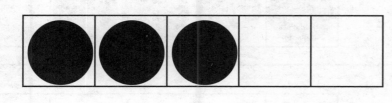

Directions Say: *How can you show that the group of gray counters is equal in number to the group of black counters? Draw lines to match the counters from one group to the other group.* 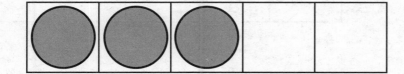 and 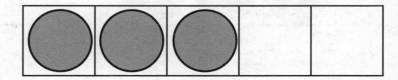 Have students draw lines to match the counters from one group to the other group. Then have them draw a circle around the groups if they are equal in number, or mark an X on the groups if they are NOT equal in number.

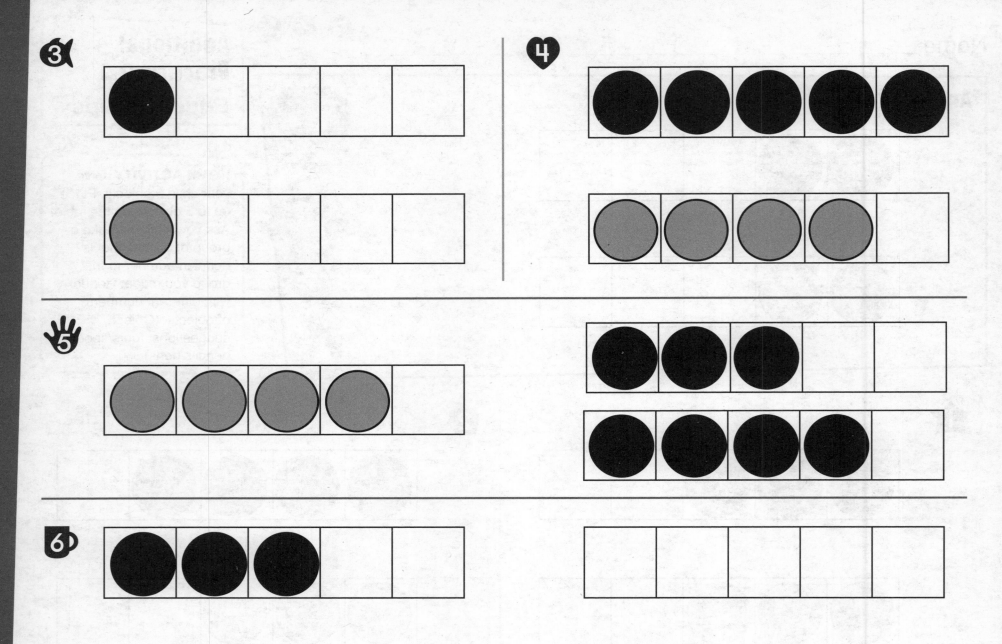

3 (bird icon)

4 (heart icon)

5 (hand icon)

6 (mug icon)

Topic 2 | Lesson I

Name _____

Another Look!

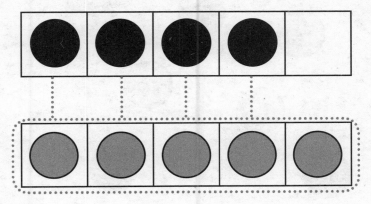

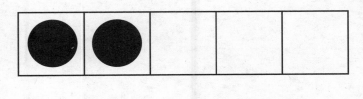

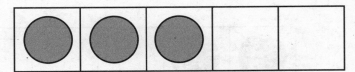

Directions Say: *How do you know which group of counters, the black or the gray, is greater in number than the other? Draw a line from each gray counter to a black counter. Draw a circle around the group that has counters left over.* ⭐ and 🍎 Have students draw lines to match the black and gray groups of counters. Have them draw a circle around the group that is greater in number than the other group, and then explain why they are correct.

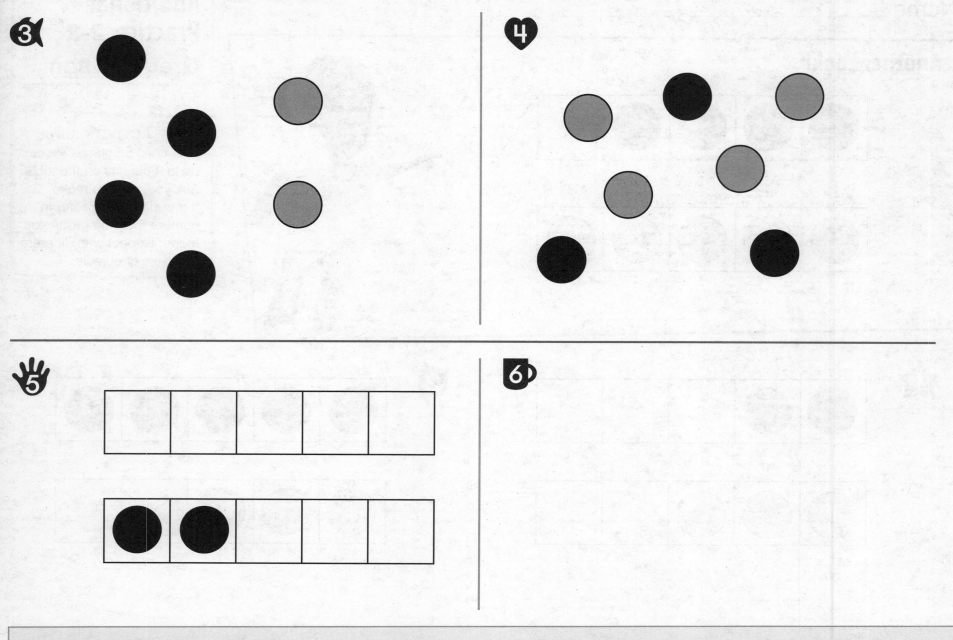

3

4

5

6

Topic 2 | Lesson 2

Name _____

Another Look!

HOME ACTIVITY Give your child 5 objects. Place at least 2 objects on the table. Ask your child to make a group that is less in number than the group you made. Repeat with different numbers of objects.

⭐1

2

Directions Say: *How do you know which group of counters, the black or the gray, is less in number than the other? Draw a line from each black counter to a gray counter. Mark an X on the group that is less in number.* ⭐ and 2 Have students draw lines to match counters from one group to the other group. Have them mark an X on the group that is less in number than the other group, and then explain why they are correct.

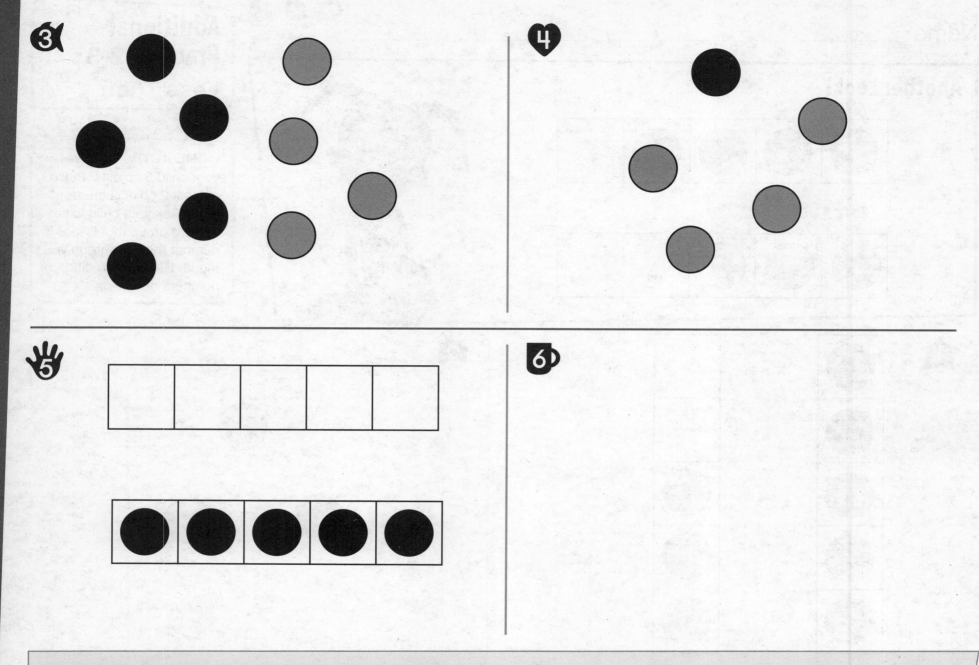

Directions ❸ and ❹ Have students draw lines to match counters from one group to the other group. Have them mark an X on the group that is less in number than the other group, and then explain why they are correct. ✋ **Higher Order Thinking** Have students draw a group of counters that is less in number than the group of black counters shown. Then have them mark an X to show the group that is less in number than the other group. ❻ **Higher Order Thinking** Have students draw two different groups of counters or objects. Have them show and explain which group is less in number than the other group.

Name _____

Another Look!

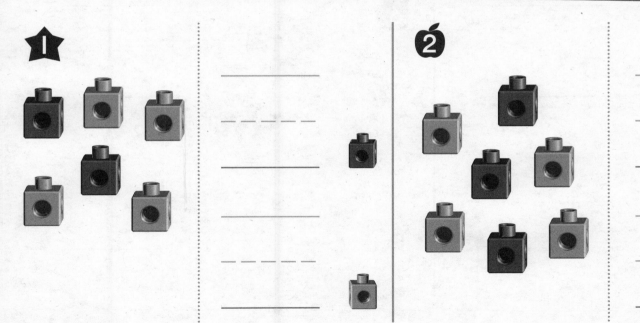

HOME ACTIVITY Gather 10 objects, such as buttons or straws. Show 4 objects randomly on a table. Ask your child to make a group of 2 objects. Have him or her write numbers to tell how many are in each group, and then explain which group is greater in number and which group is less in number.

Directions Say: *You can count the black and gray cubes to find out which group is greater in number. Count the cubes, and then write the numbers to tell how many. Draw a circle around the number that is greater than the other number and mark an X on the number that is less than the other number.* ★ and ② Have students count the cubes, write the numbers to tell how many, and then draw a circle around the number that is greater than the other number and mark an X on the number that is less than the other number.

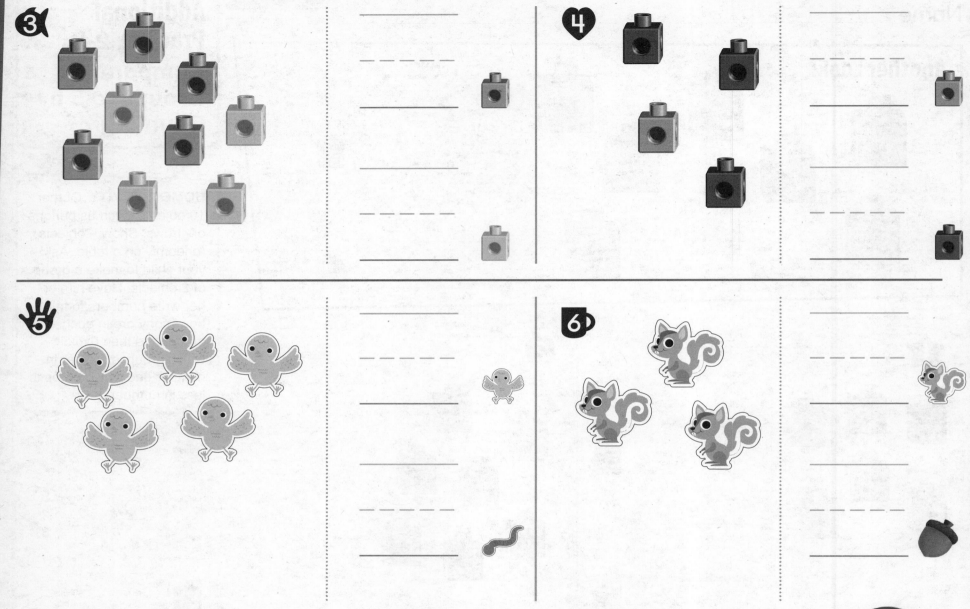

3 _[count the gray cubes]_

4 _[count the black cubes]_

5 _[bird stickers]_

6 _[squirrel stickers]_

Directions **3** and **4** Have students count the cubes, write the numbers to tell how many, and then draw a circle around the number that is greater than the other number and mark an X on the number that is less than the other number. **5 Higher Order Thinking** Have students count the bird stickers, draw a group of worms that is less in number than the group of birds shown, and then write the numbers to tell how many. **6 Higher Order Thinking** Have students count the squirrel stickers, draw a group of nuts equal in number to the group of squirrels shown, and then write the numbers to tell how many.

Name _____

Another Look!

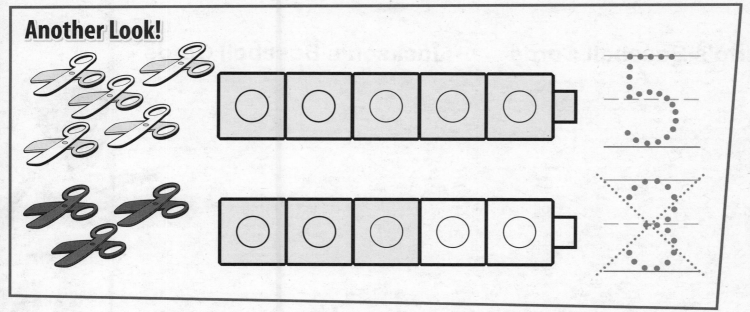

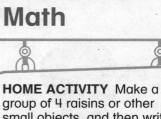

HOME ACTIVITY Make a group of 4 raisins or other small objects, and then write the number. Ask your child to make a group of 3 raisins or other small objects, and then write the number of raisins. Ask your child to use the numbers to explain which group is greater in number than the other group. Repeat with different numbers from 0 to 5.

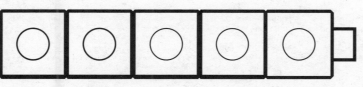

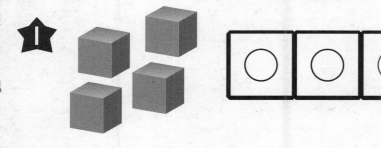

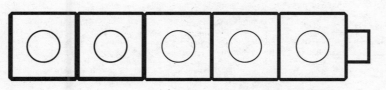

Directions Have students listen to the story. Say: *Mr. Davis has 5 white scissors and 3 black scissors for his class. Which group of scissors has less than the other group? How can you use cubes, a drawing, or numbers to find out? Create cube or object trains for each group, color the number of cubes, and then write the numbers to tell how many. Mark an X on the number that is less than the other number.* Have students repeat the steps for this story: ⭐ *Candice has 4 gray blocks and 2 white blocks. Which group of blocks is less in number than the other group?*

Marta's Baseball Cards | Jackson's Baseball Cards

Directions Read the problem aloud. Then have students use multiple problem-solving methods to solve the problem. Say: *Marta has 5 baseball cards. Jackson has less in number than Marta does. How many baseball cards could Jackson have?* ✌ **Make Sense** *What do you know about the problem? What is the number of baseball cards Jackson CANNOT have? Tell a partner and explain why.*
✸ **Model** *Use cubes, draw a picture, or use numbers to show how many baseball cards Marta has and Jackson could have.*
❹ **Explain** *Tell a partner why your work for Jackson's baseball cards is correct.*

Name _____

Another Look!

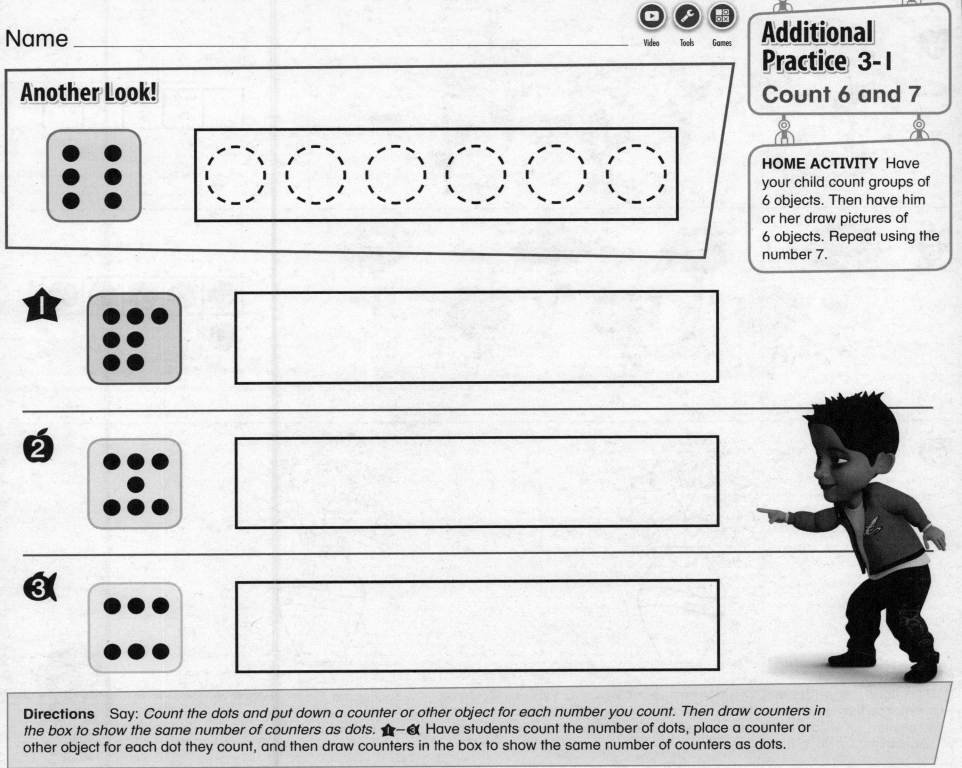

HOME ACTIVITY Have your child count groups of 6 objects. Then have him or her draw pictures of 6 objects. Repeat using the number 7.

⭐ 1

🍎 2

↪ 3

Directions Say: *Count the dots and put down a counter or other object for each number you count. Then draw counters in the box to show the same number of counters as dots.* ⭐–↪ Have students count the number of dots, place a counter or other object for each dot they count, and then draw counters in the box to show the same number of counters as dots.

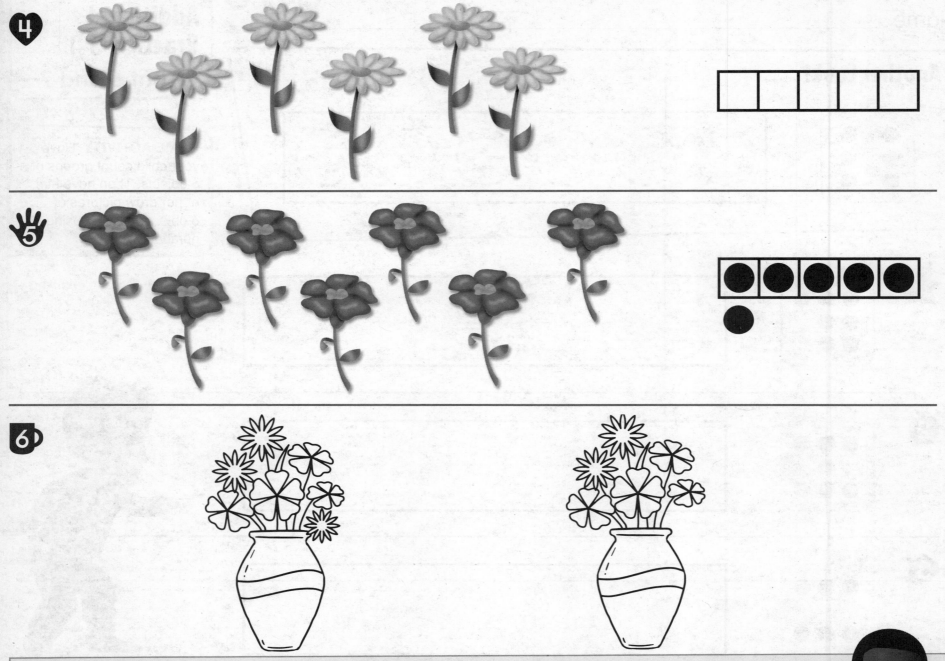

Name _____

Another Look!

●●●●●●

●●●●●●●

6 6 6

7 7 7

HOME ACTIVITY Draw groups of 6 and 7 circles on 2 index cards. Have your child write the correct number on the back of each card. Then use the cards to practice counting and reading the numbers 6 and 7.

⭐ 1 _____

_ _ _ _ _ _ _ _ _ _ _ _

🍎 2 _____

_ _ _ _ _ _ _ _ _ _ _ _

🐟 3 _____

_ _ _ _ _ _ _ _ _ _ _ _

Directions Say: *Count the counters, and then practice writing the numbers that tell how many.* ⭐–🐟 Have students count the counters, and then practice writing the number that tells how many.

6

 7

Topic 3 | Lesson 2

Name _____

Another Look!

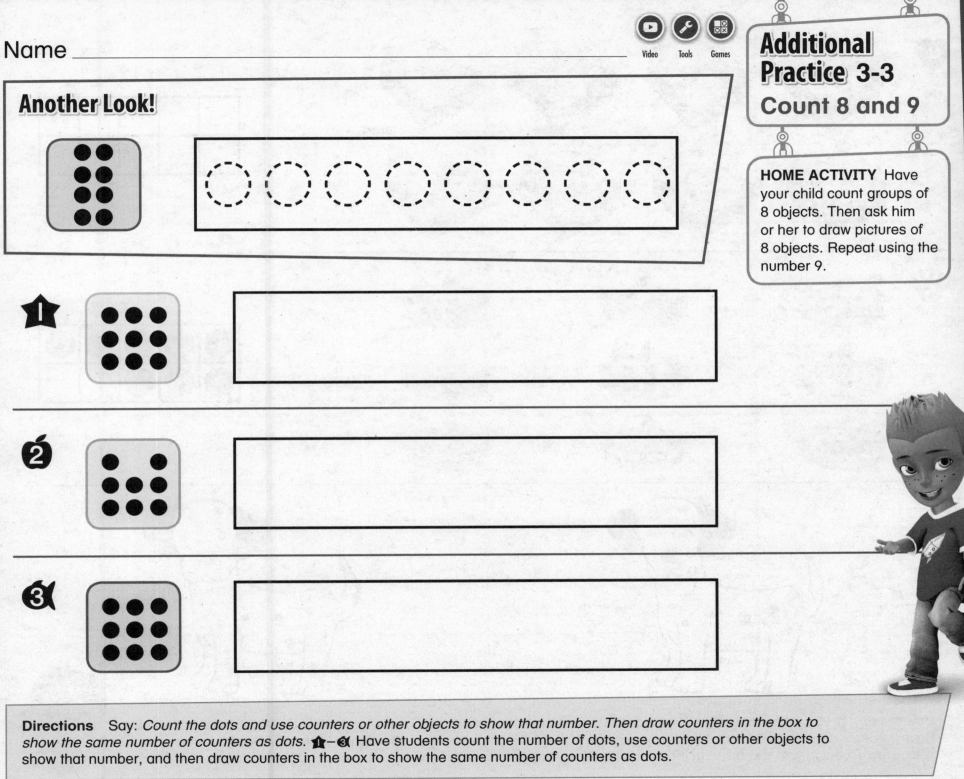

HOME ACTIVITY Have your child count groups of 8 objects. Then ask him or her to draw pictures of 8 objects. Repeat using the number 9.

Directions Say: *Count the dots and use counters or other objects to show that number. Then draw counters in the box to show the same number of counters as dots.* ★–3 Have students count the number of dots, use counters or other objects to show that number, and then draw counters in the box to show the same number of counters as dots.

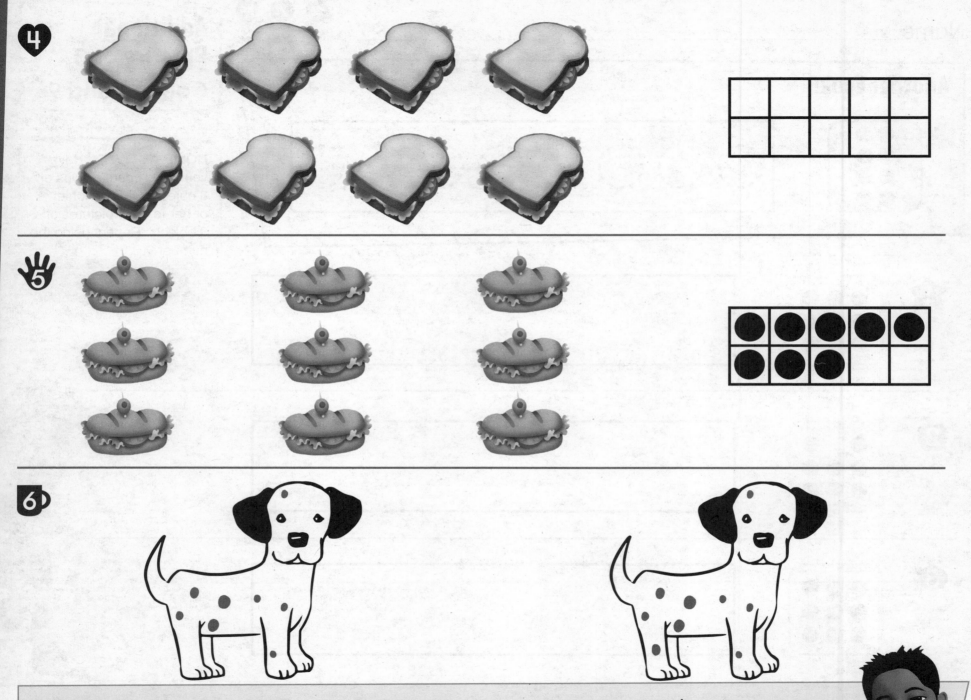

Directions ✋ Have students count the sandwiches, and then draw counters to show how many. ✋ **Higher Order Thinking** Have students draw a circle around the same number of sandwiches as counters. 🖐 **Higher Order Thinking** Have students color brown the dog with 8 spots, and then color black the dog with 9 spots.

Name _____

Another Look!

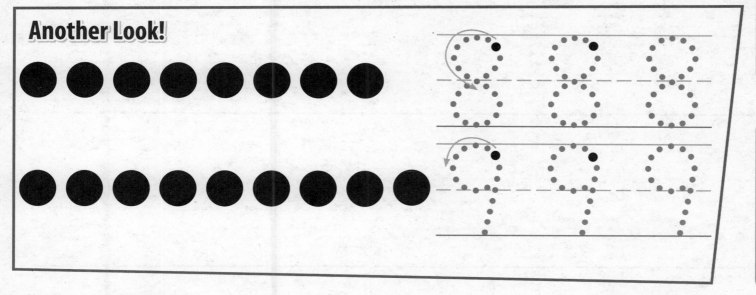

HOME ACTIVITY Draw groups of 8 and 9 circles on 2 index cards. Have your child write the correct number on the back of each card. Then use the cards to practice counting and reading the numbers 8 and 9.

Directions Say: *Count the counters, and then practice writing the number that tells how many.* ①–③ Have students count the dots, and then practice writing the number that tells how many.

8

 9

♨

🌲

Name _____

Additional Practice 3-5
Count 10

Another Look!

HOME ACTIVITY Have your child count groups of 10 objects. Then have him or her draw pictures of 10 objects.

⭐ 1

🍎 2

Directions Say: *Count the snails and use connecting cubes or other objects to show that number. Then color a connecting cube for each snail you counted to show the same number of cubes as snails.* ⭐ and 🍎 Have students count the insects, use connecting cubes or other objects to show that number, and then color a connecting cube for each insect they count to show the same number of cubes as insects.

3

 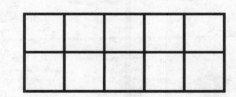

4

5

Directions ✖ Have students count the ladybugs, and then draw counters to show how many. ❤ **Higher Order Thinking** Have students draw more worms to show 10, and then draw counters to show how many. ✋ **Higher Order Thinking** Have students look at the jars, color red the jar with 9 fireflies, and then color yellow the jar with 10 fireflies.

Topic 3 | Lesson 5

Name _____

Additional Practice 3-6
Read, Make, and Write 10

Another Look!

HOME ACTIVITY Draw groups of 9 and 10 circles on 2 index cards. Have your child write the correct number on the back of each card. Then use the cards to practice counting and reading the numbers 9 and 10.

_____

_____

Directions Say: *Count the sea stars, and then write the number to tell how many.* ⭐ Have students count each group of sea stars, and then write the number to tell how many.

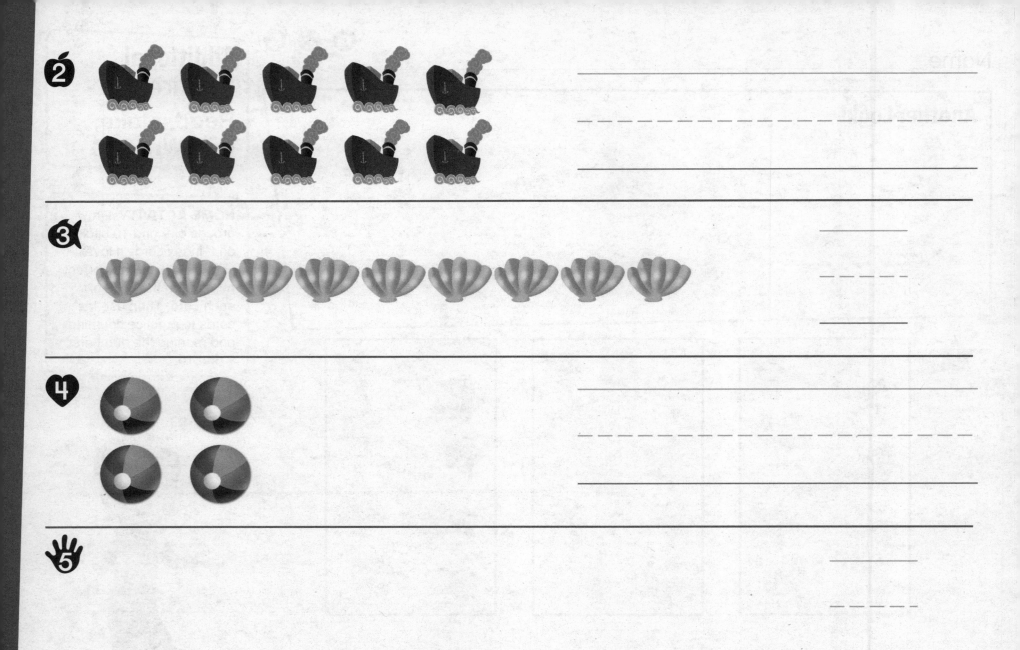

2

3

4

5

Directions Have students: **2** count the boats, and then practice writing the number that tells how many; **3** count the shells, and then write the number to tell how many. **4** **Higher Order Thinking** Have students draw more beach balls to show 10, and then practice writing the number 10. **5** **Higher Order Thinking** Have students draw 10 shells, and then write the number to tell how many.

Name _____

Another Look!

0   1   2

HOME ACTIVITY Write a number on a piece of paper and have your child write the number that is 1 greater. Then write another number and have your child write the number that is 1 less. Repeat with other numbers.

⭐ 1   [5 dots]   _ _ _ _   **6**   [6 dots]   _ _ _ _

🍎 2   [4 dots]   _ _ _ _   **5**   [5 dots]   _ _ _ _

🐟 3 | 10 | 8 | 7 | 9 | _ _ _ _ _ _ _ _

❤️ 4 | 3 | 2 | 1 | 0 | _ _ _ _ _ _ _ _

Directions Say: *Write the numbers that are 1 less than and 1 greater than 1. Count the numbers aloud.* Then have students: ⭐ and 🍎 count to find the number that is 1 less than and 1 greater than the given number, and then write the numbers; 🐟 and ❤️ compare the number cards, write the smallest number, and then count forward and write the number that is 1 greater than the number before.

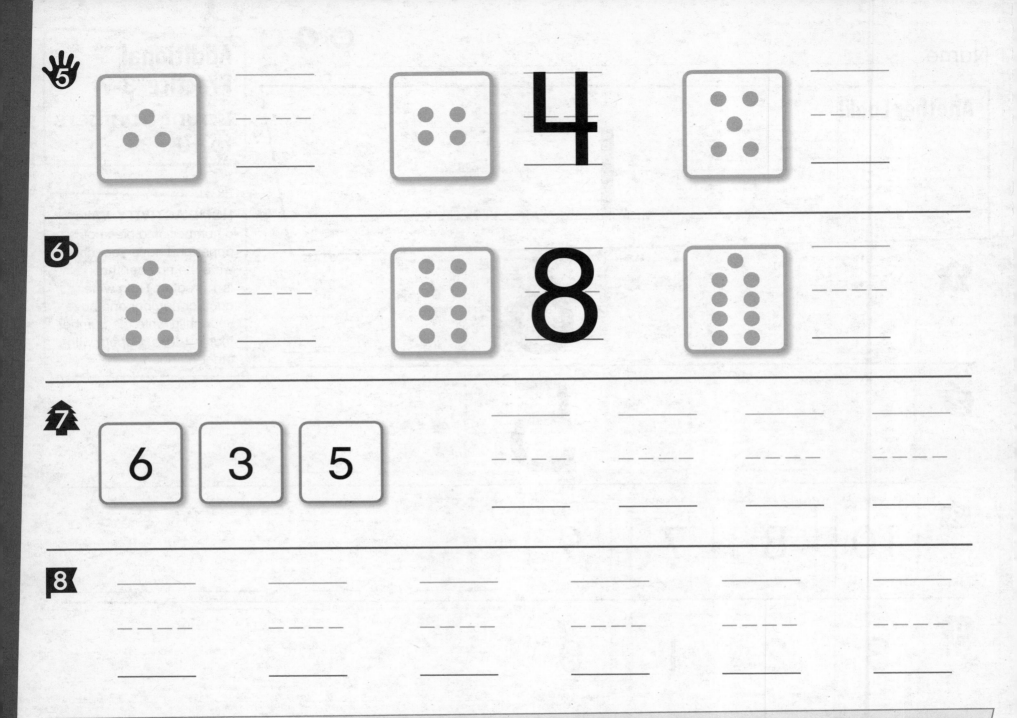

44 forty-four

Topic 3 | Lesson 7

Name _____

 Video Tools Games

Additional Practice 3-8
Look For and Use Structure

Another Look!

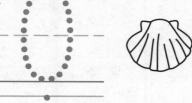 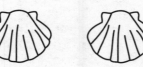

  shells shells shells

 shells shells shells shells

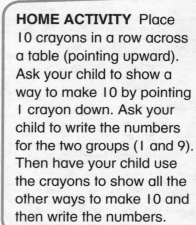

HOME ACTIVITY Place 10 crayons in a row across a table (pointing upward). Ask your child to show a way to make 10 by pointing 1 crayon down. Ask your child to write the numbers for the two groups (1 and 9). Then have your child use the crayons to show all the other ways to make 10 and then write the numbers.

 1

Directions Say: *You can make a number pattern to show different ways to make groups of 4 shells. First, you can show 0 shells in color and 4 white shells. Next, you can color to show 1 shell in color and 3 white shells. Write the numbers.* 1 Say: *Show three other ways to make 4.* Have students color the shells red and yellow to complete the pattern showing the ways to make 4, and then write the numbers. Have them describe the pattern.

Topic 3 | Lesson 8   Go Online | SavvasRealize.com   forty-five **45**

Name _____

Another Look!

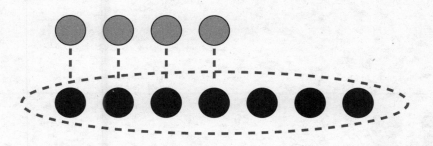

Directions Say: *Compare the groups by matching the counters in each group. Draw a circle around the group of counters that is greater in number than the other.* Have students: ⭐ compare the groups and draw a circle around the group of counters that is greater in number; 🍎 and 🐟 compare the groups and draw a circle around the group of counters that is less in number.

4

 5

 6

 7

Directions Have students: **4** compare the groups and draw a circle around the group of chicks that is greater in number than the other group; **5** compare the groups and draw a circle around the group of chicks that is less in number than the other group. **6 Higher Order Thinking** Have students draw a group of buckets that is less in number than the group shown. **7 Higher Order Thinking** Have students draw a group of counters, and then draw a second group of counters that is greater in number than the first group of counters.

48 forty-eight

Topic 4 | Lesson 1

Name _____

Another Look!

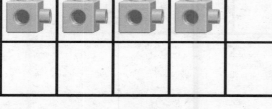

HOME ACTIVITY Show a group of up to 10 objects, such as buttons. Ask your child to show a group of objects that is greater in number than your group. Repeat with a group that is less in number than your group of objects.

1

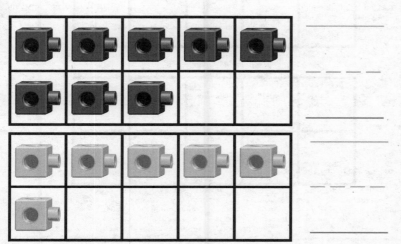

2

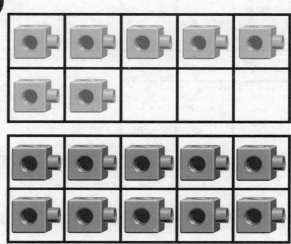

Directions Say: *Count the cubes in each group, write the number to tell how many, and then draw a circle around the number that is greater than the other number.* **1** and **2** Have students count the cubes in each group, write the number to tell how many, and then mark an X on the number that is less than the other number.

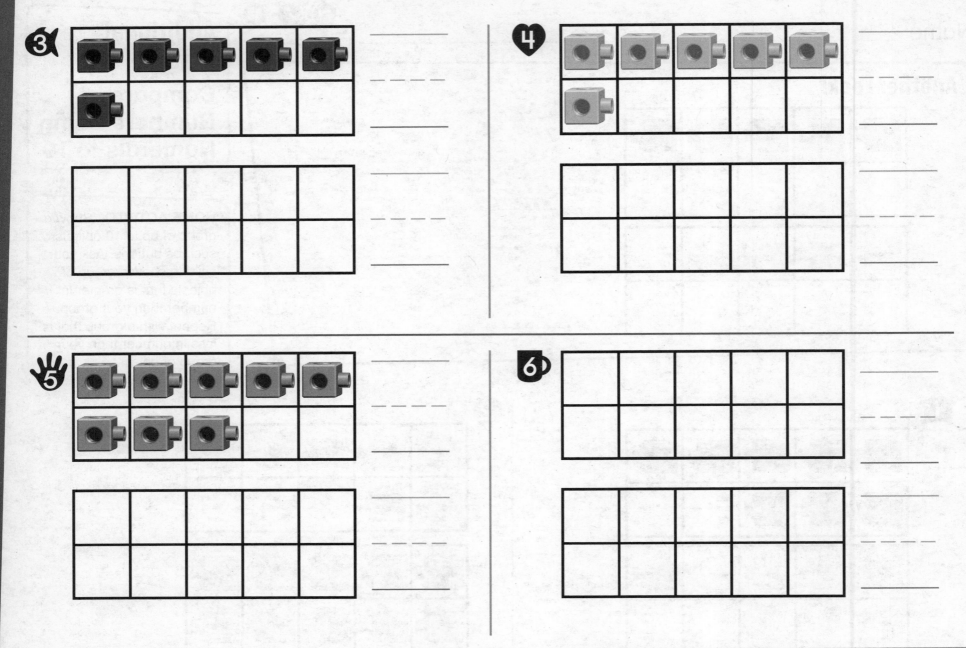

3

4

5

6

50 fifty

Topic 4 | Lesson 2

Name _____

Another Look!

1 2 3 4 5 6 7 8 9 10

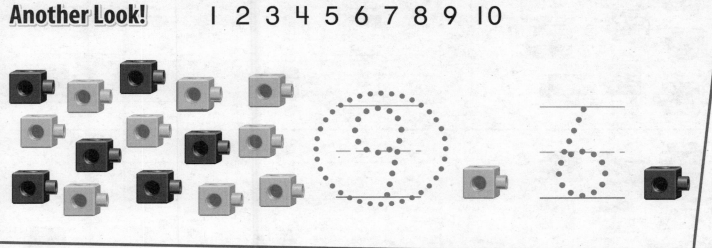

HOME ACTIVITY Shake up to 10 pennies and up to 10 nickels in your hand. Let them fall in a random group on the table. Have your child count the number of each coin, write the numbers, and then hold up the coin of the number that is greater. Repeat with different numbers of coins. Vary the activity by also asking them to hold up the coin of the number that is less, or hold up both if the numbers are equal.

1 2 3 4 5 6 7 8 9 10

⭐ 1

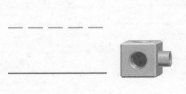

Directions Say: *Count the black cubes. Then count the gray cubes. Write the numbers to tell how many of each color. Draw a circle around the number that is greater than the other number. Use the number sequence to help find the answer.* ⭐ Have students count the number of each color cube, write the numbers to tell how many, and then draw a circle around the number that is greater than the other number. Use the number sequence to help find the answer.

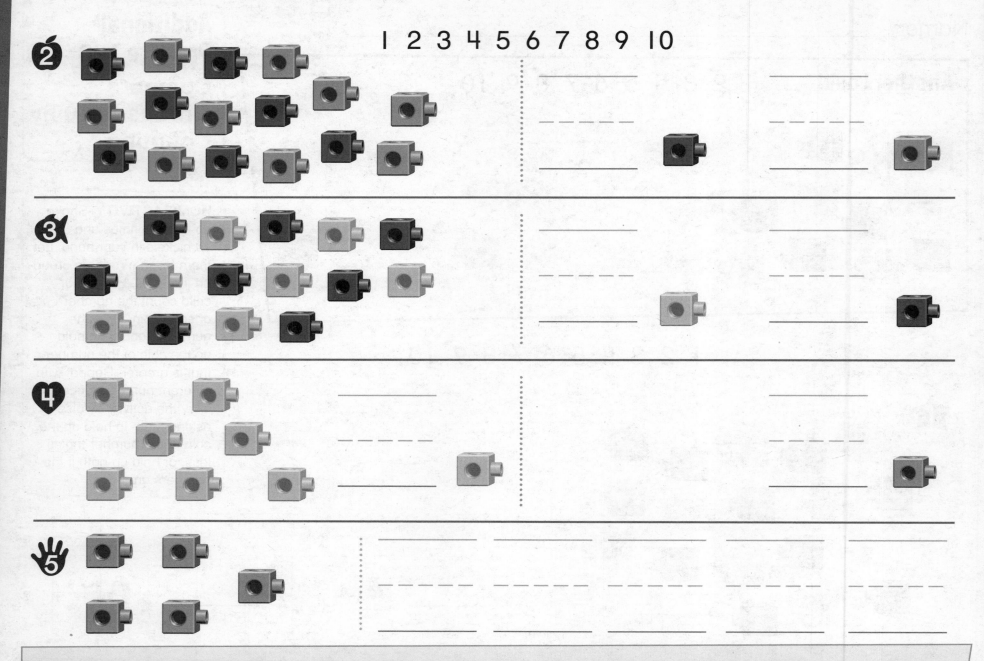

1 2 3 4 5 6 7 8 9 10

Topic 4 | Lesson 3

Directions Have students count the number of each color cube, write the numbers to tell how many, and then: ❷ mark an X on the number that is less than the other number; ❸ draw a circle around both numbers if they are equal, or mark an X on both numbers if they are NOT equal. ❹ Have students draw a group of black cubes that is equal to the number of cubes shown. ❺ **Higher Order Thinking** Have students count the cubes, and then write all the numbers that are greater than the number of cubes shown up to 10. Use the number sequence to help find the answer for each problem.

Name _____

Another Look!

9

7

HOME ACTIVITY Give your child 10 pennies and 10 nickels. Write two numbers on a sheet of paper and ask your child to show the two numbers using the coins. Then have your child draw a circle around the number that is greater, mark an X on the number that is less, or draw a circle around both numbers if they are equal.

★ 1

6

7

🍎 2

8

6

Directions Say: *Draw counters in the ten-frames to help find the answer. Then compare the numbers and draw a circle around the number that is greater than the other number.* Have students draw counters in the ten-frames to help find the answer, and then: ★ draw a circle around the number that is greater than the other number; 🍎 mark an X on the number that is less than the other number.

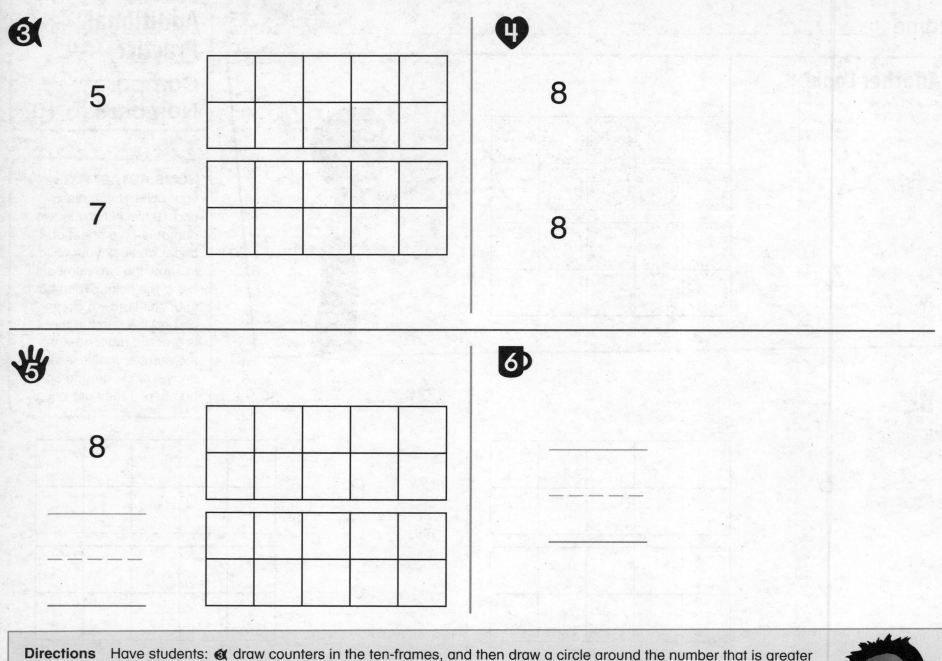

3 5

7

4 8

8

5 8

_ _ _ _ _

_ _ _ _

6 _____

- - - - -

_____

Name _____

Another Look!

7

HOME ACTIVITY Give your child 10 crayons. Then place a row of 8 paper clips, or other small objects, on a table. Ask your child to make a row of crayons that is 1 greater in number than the number of paper clips and then tell how many. Repeat with other numbers.

★ 1

🍎 2

🐟 3

Directions Say: *You can show 1 more than the group of butterflies using counters. Use reasoning to find the number that is 1 greater than the number of butterflies shown. Draw counters to show your answer, and then write the number.* Have students explain their reasoning. Have students: ★ and 🍎 *use reasoning to find the number that is 1 greater than the spiders or butterflies shown. Draw counters to show the answer, and then write the number;* 🐟 *use counters to find the number that is 2 greater than the number of spiders shown, draw the counters, and then write the number.* Have students explain their reasoning.

Comparing Goldfish

· ·

· ·

Directions Read the problem aloud. Then have students use multiple problem-solving methods to solve the problem. Say: *Alex has 7 goldfish. Marta has 1 more goldfish than Alex. Emily has 1 more goldfish than Marta. How many goldfish does Emily have?* ❹ **Generalize** *What part of the problem repeats? How does that help to solve the problem?* ✋ **Use Tools** *What tool can you use to help solve the problem? Use the tool to find the number of goldfish Emily has.* ❻ **Make Sense** *Which person should have a number of goldfish greater than the others? How do you know?*

Name _____

Another Look!

HOME ACTIVITY Show your child two categories of objects that are different in at least one way. For example, show 6 coins that are silver and 4 coins that are not silver. Ask your child to classify the objects and explain how he or she classified them. Repeat the activity with other categories using up to 10 objects.

Directions Say: *You can classify objects into categories and tell how you classified them. Draw a circle around the animals that are adults, and then mark an X on the animals that are NOT adults.* ⭐ Have students draw a circle around the animals that have beaks, and then mark an X on the animals that do NOT have beaks.

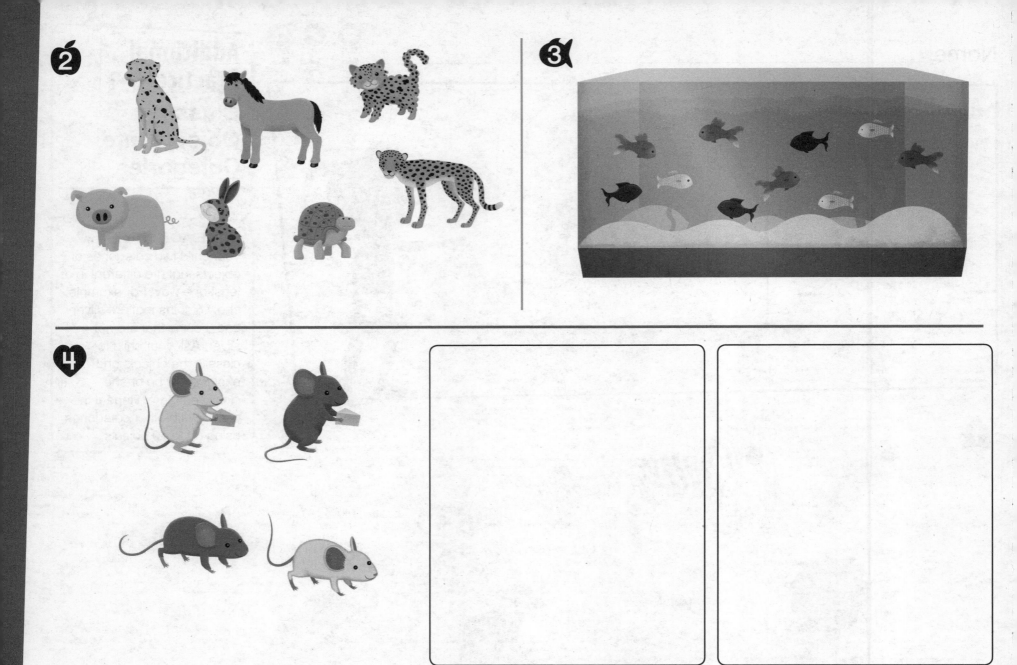

2

3

4

Topic 5 | Lesson 1

Name _____

Another Look!

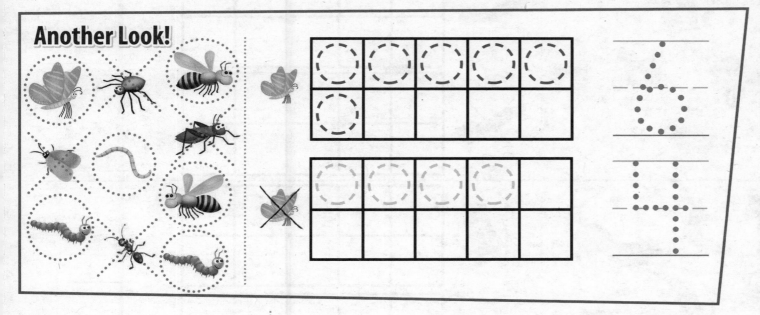

HOME ACTIVITY Show your child a group of 12 or fewer objects that are different in at least one way. For example, show 4 blue buttons, 3 brown buttons, and 5 white buttons. Arrange the objects in a random order. Ask your child to draw lines to count the buttons that are white and the buttons that are NOT white. Then have your child write numbers for his or her lines. Repeat the activity with other categories of up to 12 objects.

★1

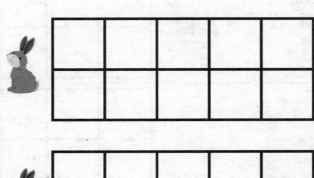

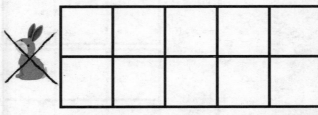

Directions Say: *You can use counters and a ten-frame to sort objects and count how many objects are in each category. Draw a circle around each animal that has stripes. Draw that many red counters in the top ten-frame, and then write the number to tell how many. Mark an X on each animal that does NOT have stripes. Draw that many yellow counters in the bottom ten-frame, and then write the number to tell how many.* ★ Have students draw a circle around each animal that has 4 legs, draw that many red counters in the top ten-frame, and then write the number to tell how many. Have students mark an X on each animal that does NOT have 4 legs, draw that many yellow counters in the bottom ten-frame, and then write the number to tell how many.

Directions Have students draw a circle around animals in one category, draw that many red counters in the top ten-frame, and then write the number to tell how many. Then have them mark an X on animals in the other category, draw that many yellow counters in the bottom ten-frame, and then write the number to tell how many. ❷ Categories: animals that have wings, animals that do NOT have wings ❸ Categories: dogs that are puppies, dogs that are NOT puppies. ❹ **Higher Order Thinking** Say: *Gretchen is going to put 1 more striped fish in the aquarium. Draw red counters in the top ten-frame to show how many striped fish will be in the aquarium. Write the number to tell how many.* Have students mark an X on the fish that are NOT striped, draw yellow counters in the bottom ten-frame, and then write the number to tell how many.

60 sixty

Topic 5 | Lesson 2

Name _____

Video   Tools   Games

Another Look!

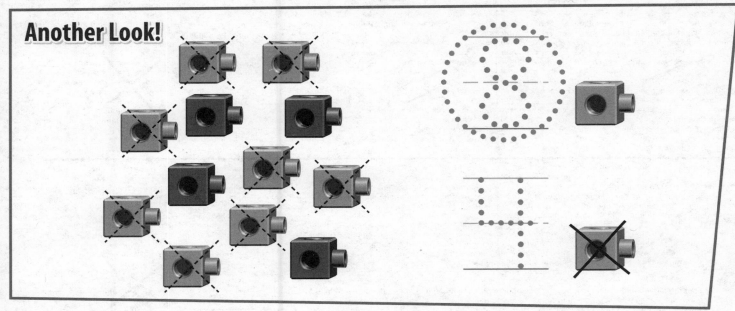

HOME ACTIVITY Show your child a group of 12 or fewer objects that are different in at least one way. For example, show 5 spoons and 6 forks. Arrange them in a random order. Ask your child to count the objects that are forks and the objects that are NOT forks, tell which category has a greater number of objects, and then explain how he or she knows. Repeat with another group of objects and have your child tell you which category has a number of objects that is less than the other category.

★1

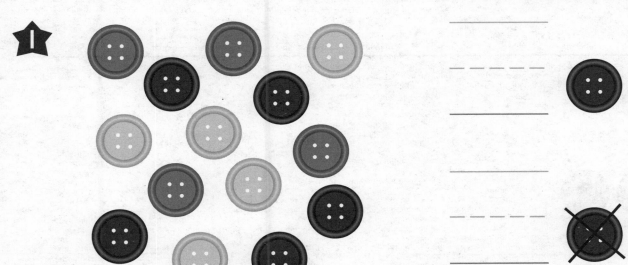

Directions Say: *Mark an X on the gray cubes, count the gray cubes, and then write how many. Count the cubes that are NOT gray, and then write how many. Draw a circle around the number that is greater than the other number. Tell how you know.* ★ Have students mark an X on each black button, count them, and then write how many. Have students count the buttons that are NOT black, write how many, and then draw a circle around the number that is less than the other number. Have them tell how they know.

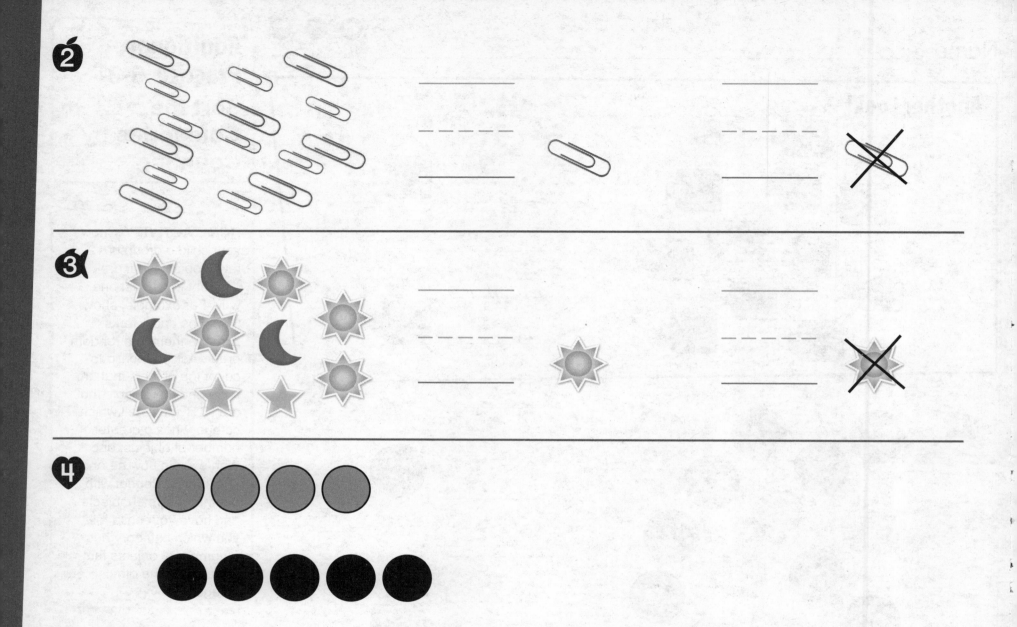

2

3

4

Name _____

Additional Practice 5-4
Critique Reasoning

Another Look!

 **6**   **7**

(yes)   no

⭐ **5**   **8**

yes   no

HOME ACTIVITY Show your child a group of up to 19 objects that are different in at least one way; for example, 9 plates and 8 cups. Arrange the objects in a random order and make a statement comparing the objects. For example, say: *The category of plates is greater in number than the category of cups.* Ask your child whether your statement makes sense and to explain how he or she knows. Repeat the activity with other groups of objects and statements that either make sense or do NOT make sense.

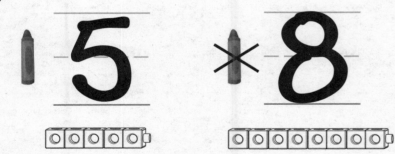

Directions Say: *Tanya used cubes to show how many crayons are white and how many crayons are NOT white. She says that the category of white crayons is less in number than the category of crayons that are NOT white. Does her answer make sense? Draw a circle around* yes *or* no. *Then use the sorting and counting of each category to explain your reasoning.* ⭐ Say: *Jared says that the category of gray crayons is greater in number than the category that is NOT gray. Does his answer make sense?* Have students draw a circle around *yes* or *no*, and then use the sorting and counting of each category to explain their reasoning.

Directions Read the problem aloud. Then have students use multiple problem-solving methods to solve the problem. Say: *Carlos says that if there were 3 more gray dogs, then the category of gray dogs would be greater in number than the category of dogs that are NOT gray. Does his answer make sense?* ❷ **Model** *How can you show whether or not his answer makes sense? Use tools or draw a picture to show how many gray dogs there would be if 3 more gray dogs join the category.* ❸ **Be Precise** *Is the number of gray dogs now greater than the number of dogs that are NOT gray?* ❹ **Critique Reasoning** *Use the sorting and counting of each category to explain your reasoning.*

Name _____

Another Look!

2 and 6 is 8 in all.

HOME ACTIVITY Give your child 10 pennies, and then say a number between 2 and 10. Ask your child to make that number with two groups, and then clap and knock to show you the two parts. For example, if you say 8, your child can make a group of 5 pennies and a group of 3 pennies. He or she will clap 5 times and knock 3 times.

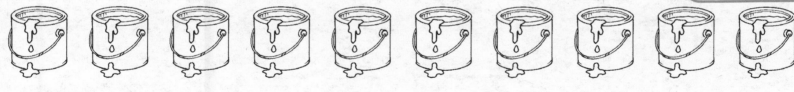

5 and 5 is ____ in all.

Directions Say: *There are 2 yellow paint buckets. There are 6 orange paint buckets. How many paint buckets are there in all?* Model how to clap and knock each part, how to show the parts with fingers, and how to think of the parts with a mental image to find the whole. Then have students color the number of each part, and then write the number to tell how many in all. ⭐ Have students listen to the story, and then do all of the following to show each part to find how many in all: clap and knock, hold up fingers, and give an explanation of a mental image. Ask them to color the number of each part, and then write the number to tell how many in all. *Mattias has 5 red paint buckets. He has 5 blue paint buckets. How many paint buckets does he have in all?*

$$2 \text{ and } 4 \text{ is } \underline{} \text{ in all.}$$

$$10 \text{ is } \underline{} \text{ and } \underline{}.$$

Directions ❷ Have students listen to the story, and then do all of the following to show each part to find how many in all: clap and knock, hold up fingers, and give an explanation of a mental image. Ask them to color the number of each part, and then write the number to tell how many in all. *Shruthi has 2 green paint buckets. She has 4 blue paint buckets. How many paint buckets does she have in all?* ❸ **Higher Order Thinking** Have students listen to the story, color the paint buckets to show the parts, and then write the numbers to tell how many of each. *Freddy has 10 paint buckets. He fills some with purple paint. He fills the others with red paint. How many does he fill with each color?*

Name _____

Video Tools Games

Additional
Practice 6-2
Represent
Addition as
Adding To

Another Look!

5

6 7 8

5 ___ and ___ 3 ___ is ___ 8 ___ .

HOME ACTIVITY Have
your child model counting
on with paper clips or
pennies. For example,
ask your child to make a
group of 4 paper clips and
a group of 3 paper clips.
Have your child count the
first group, and then from
that number, count on the
number of paper clips in all.

★1

②

___ and ___ is ___ .   ___ and ___ is ___ .

Directions Say: *Marta has some cubes. Then she gets some more. You can write numbers to show how Marta counts on to add more to the group of cubes. Then write an addition sentence to tell how many in all.* ★ and ② Say: *Daniel has some cubes. Then he gets some more.* Have students count on to add to the group of cubes, and then write an addition sentence to tell how many in all.

3

_____ and _____ is _____ .

4

_____ and _____ is _____ .

5

_____ and _____ is _____ .

6

_____ and _____ is _____ 6 .

Directions **3** and **4** Have students write the numbers to tell how many to add to the group when more boats come, and then write how many there are in all. **5** **Higher Order Thinking** Have students listen to the story, draw the other group of counters, and then write an addition sentence to match the story. *There are some boats in the water. 6 more boats come. There are 9 boats in all.* **6** **Higher Order Thinking** Have students draw a group of up to 6 connecting cubes. Then have them draw the number of cubes they need to add to equal 6, and then complete the addition sentence.

Name _____

Additional Practice 6-3
Represent Addition as Putting Together

Another Look!

1 and 4 is 5.

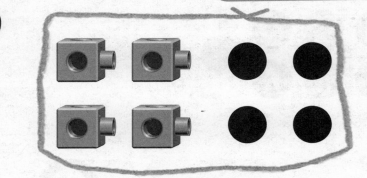

HOME ACTIVITY Take turns choosing a problem on this page and making up a number story about it. One person tells the story, and the other person writes the complete addition sentence. For example, 1 and 4 is 5.

⭐ 1

_____ and _____ is _____.

🍎 2

_____ and _____ is _____.

Directions Say: *How many cubes are there? How many counters are there? When you put the math tools together with yarn, you can count them all to find how many. Write how many of each math tool there is, and then write an addition sentence to tell how many in all.*
⭐ and 🍎 Have students write the numbers to tell how many of each math tool there is, and then write an addition sentence to tell how many in all.

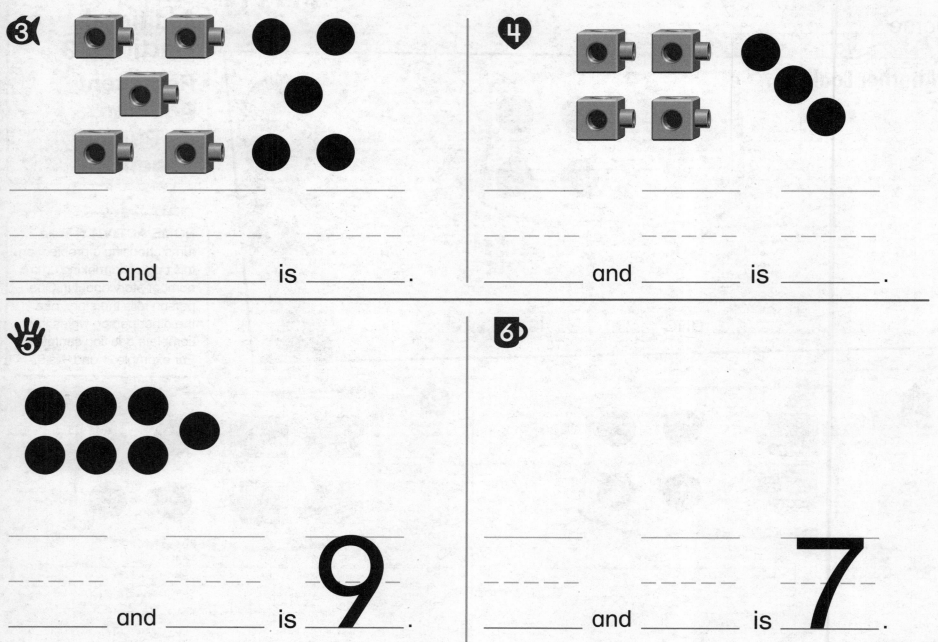

3 _____ _____

_____ and _____ is _____ .

4 _____ _____

_____ and _____ is _____ .

5 _____

_____ and _____ is **9** .

6 _____

_____ and _____ is **7** .

Topic 6 | **Lesson 3**

Name _____

Another Look!

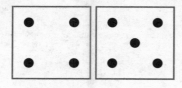

4   and   5   is   9.

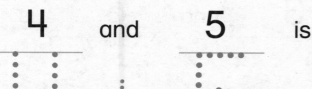

HOME ACTIVITY Make a set of number cards from 1 to 5. Shuffle them and place them facedown on a table. Take turns picking 2 number cards and finding the sum of the two numbers. Work with your child to write an equation using the plus and equal signs.

⭐ 1

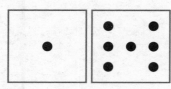

1   and   7   is   8.

_____

2️⃣

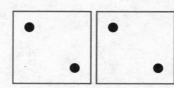

2   and   2   is   4.

_____

Directions Say: *What numbers do the dot cards show? Write the numbers, the plus sign, the equal sign, and the sum to show addition.* ⭐ and 2️⃣ Have students add the groups to find the sum, and then write an equation to show the addition.

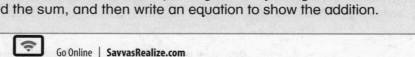

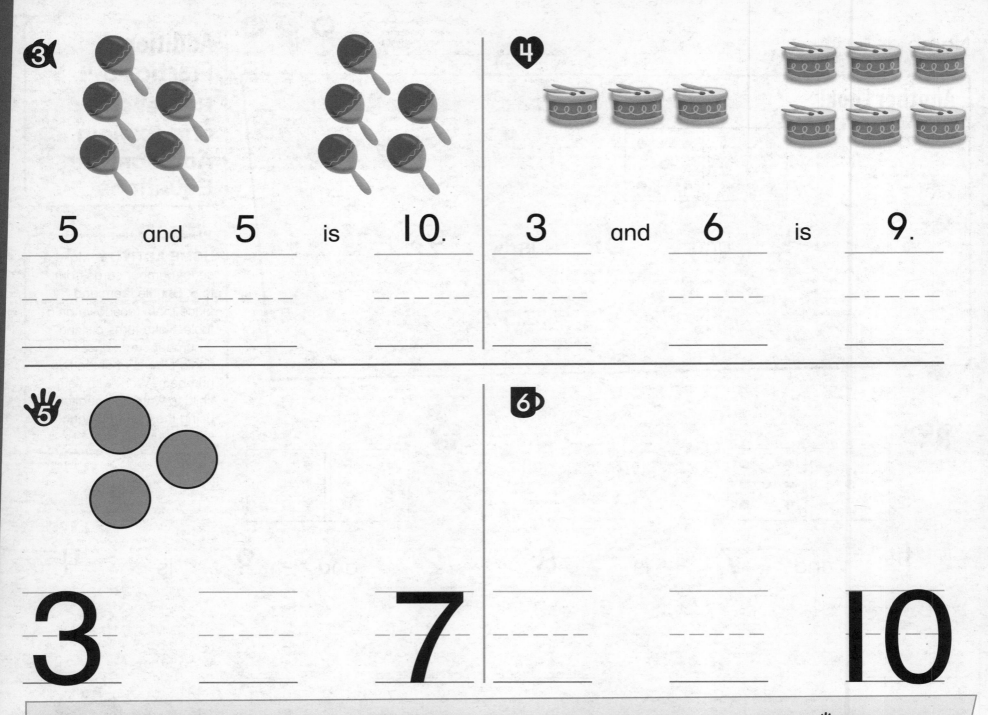

3

5 and 5 is 10.

___ ___ ___

4

3 and 6 is 9.

___ ___ ___

5

3 ___ 7

6

___ 10

Name _____

Another Look!

5 + 2 = 7

HOME ACTIVITY Give your child two numbers up to 10. Ask him or her to tell an addition story using the numbers. Repeat with different numbers.

★ 1

★ 2

Directions Say: *How can you explain the equation* 5 + 2 = 7? Guide students to tell an addition story using the equation. Have students listen to the story, use connecting cubes to show the addition, draw a picture, and write an equation. ★ *4 fish swim in the water. 6 more join them. How many fish are there in all?* ★ *2 sea stars lie on a rock. 3 more join them. How many sea stars are there in all?*

3 ✒️

4 💗

5 ✋

6 ☕

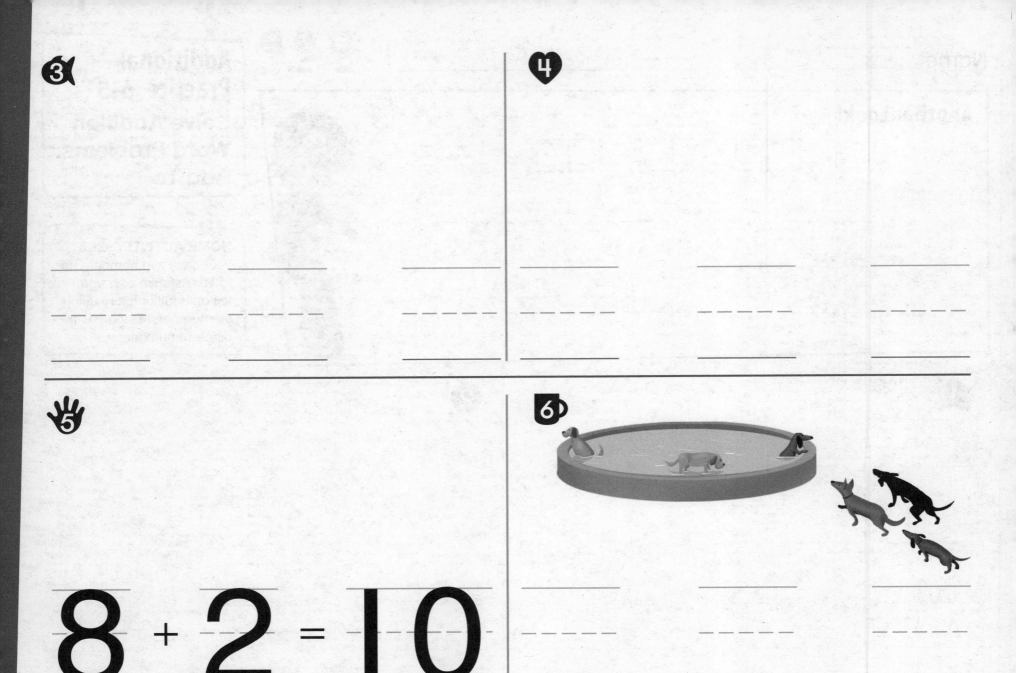

$$8 + 2 = 10$$

Directions Have students listen to the story, use a model to show the addition, draw a picture, and write an equation. **3** *4 flowers grow in a pond. 3 more grow. How many flowers are there in all?* **4** *2 butterflies sit on a bush. 6 more join them. How many butterflies are there in all?* **5 Higher Order Thinking** Have students tell an addition story that matches the equation, and then draw a picture to show what is happening. **6 Higher Order Thinking** Have students tell an addition story that matches the picture, and then write an equation to match.

Name _____

Another Look!

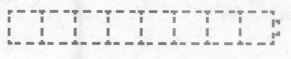

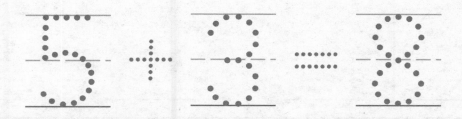

$5 + 3 = 8$

HOME ACTIVITY Give your child a group of 2 pennies and a group of 3 pennies and ask: *How can you tell there are 5 coins in all?* Encourage your child to show how he or she knows by lining up the coins and using words to describe how to add the groups together.

_____   _____

_____   _____

_____   _____

Directions Say: *How can you explain the equation* $5 + 3 = 8$? Guide students to connect cubes or put together other objects to model the addition. Encourage students to explain their thinking. Have students listen to each story, draw a picture to show what is happening, and then write an equation. ★ *There are 2 cherries on a plate and 3 cherries in a bowl. How many cherries are there in all?* ② *There are 4 apples on the counter and 6 apples in a bag. How many apples are there in all?*

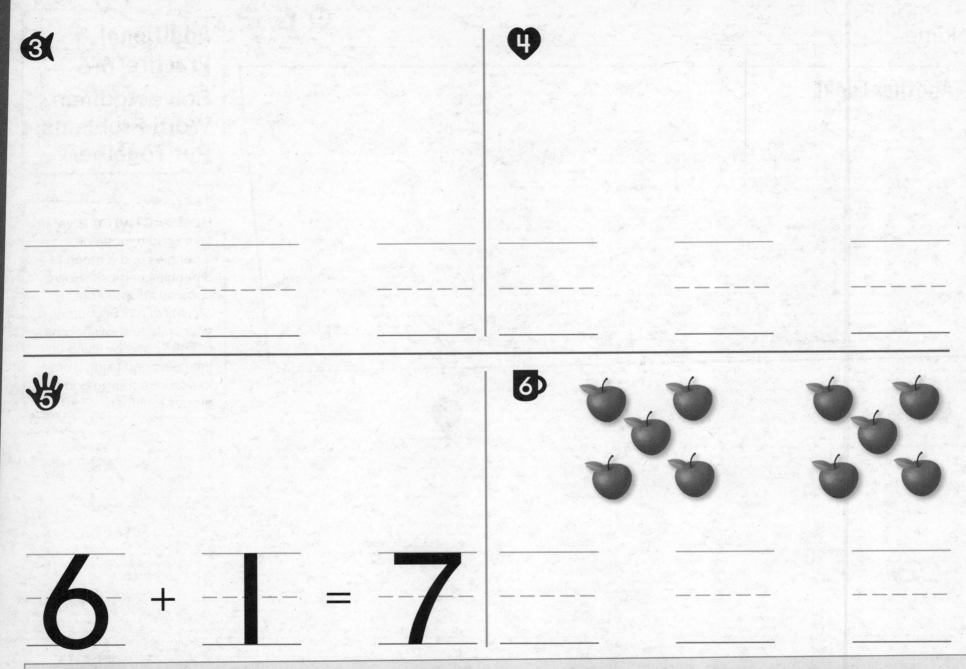

3

4

5

$$6 + 1 = 7$$

6

Directions Have students listen to each story, draw a picture to show what is happening, and then write an equation. **3** *There are 3 cardinals and 5 robins sitting on a tree branch. How many birds are there in all?* **4** *There are 4 rabbits and 4 squirrels looking for food by a tree. How many animals are there in all?* **5** **Higher Order Thinking** Have students tell an addition story that matches the equation, and then draw a picture to show what is happening. **6** **Higher Order Thinking** Have students tell an addition story about the groups of apples, and then write an equation to tell how many in all.

Topic 6 | Lesson 6

Video Tools Games

Additional Practice 6-7

Use Patterns to Develop Fluency in Addition

Another Look!

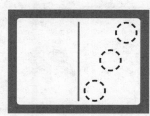  

$$0 + 3 = 3$$

HOME ACTIVITY Give your child an equation with sums up to 5. Ask him or her to write the matching pair. For example, write *1 + 3 = 4*. Your child should write *3 + 1 = 4*.

 ⭐

❷

Directions Say: *Draw counters to show how to make 3. Write an equation to match the counters.* ⭐ and ❷ Have students draw counters to continue the pattern of ways to make 3, and then write an equation to match the counters.

3

4

5

3

4

6

78 seventy-eight

Topic 6 | Lesson 7

Name _____

Another Look!

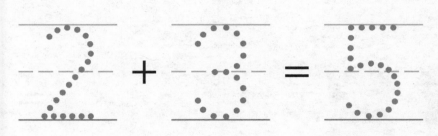

$$2 + 3 = 5$$

 1

___ + ___ = ___

2

___ + ___ = ___

Directions Say: *Carlos finds 2 apples on a tree. Then he finds 3 more on the ground. How many apples does Carlos find in all? Draw the apples, count the apples to find out how many in all, and then write an equation.* Have students listen to each story, and then draw a picture to model what is happening. Then have them write an equation and explain their answer. **1** *There are 4 balls in the box. Paolo puts 1 more ball in the box. How many balls are there in all?* **2** *Layla has 3 oranges on a plate. Bryce has 3 oranges on a plate. How many oranges do Layla and Bryce have in all?*

_____ = _____ + _____

_____ = _____ + _____

Directions Read the problem aloud. Then have students use multiple problem-solving methods to solve the problem. _Daniel and Carlos each receive 3 flowers. They each put the flowers into vases. Daniel arranges his flowers in a different way than Carlos. Show how the students could have arranged the flowers._ ❸ **Reasoning** _What do you know? How many flowers does each student have?_ ❹ **Model** _Use cubes, draw a picture, or use numbers to show two different ways that the students could have arranged their flowers. Then write the equation for each model._ ✋ **Explain** _How do you know that your models are correct? Explain your answer._

 Topic 6 | Lesson 8

Name _____

Another Look!

4 are left.

_____ are left.

HOME ACTIVITY Put up to 10 coins on a napkin and have your child count them. Then move some of the coins off of the napkin. Ask: *How many coins are left on the napkin?* Repeat the activity using a different number of coins.

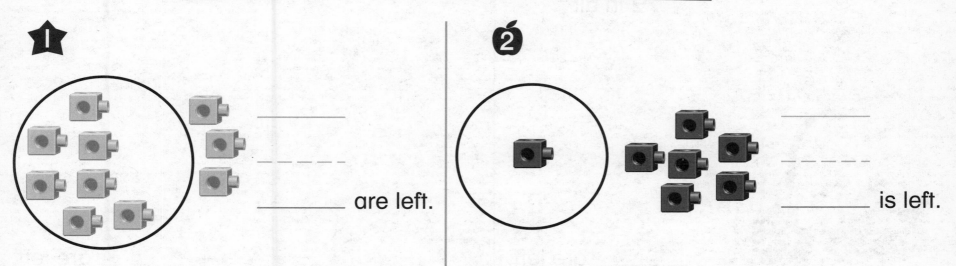

⭐ 1 _____ are left.

🍎 2 _____ is left.

Directions Say: *Carlos puts 8 cubes inside a circle. He moves 4 of them outside the circle.* Model how to explain a mental image, how to act it out with objects, and how to hold up fingers to show how many cubes are left inside the circle. Have students listen to the story, and then do all of the following to find how many are left: give an explanation of a mental image, use objects to act it out, and hold up fingers. Have them write the number to tell how many are left. ⭐ *Carlos puts 10 cubes inside a circle. He moves 3 of them out. How many cubes are left?* 🍎 *Carlos puts 7 cubes inside a circle. He moves 6 of them out. How many cubes are left?*

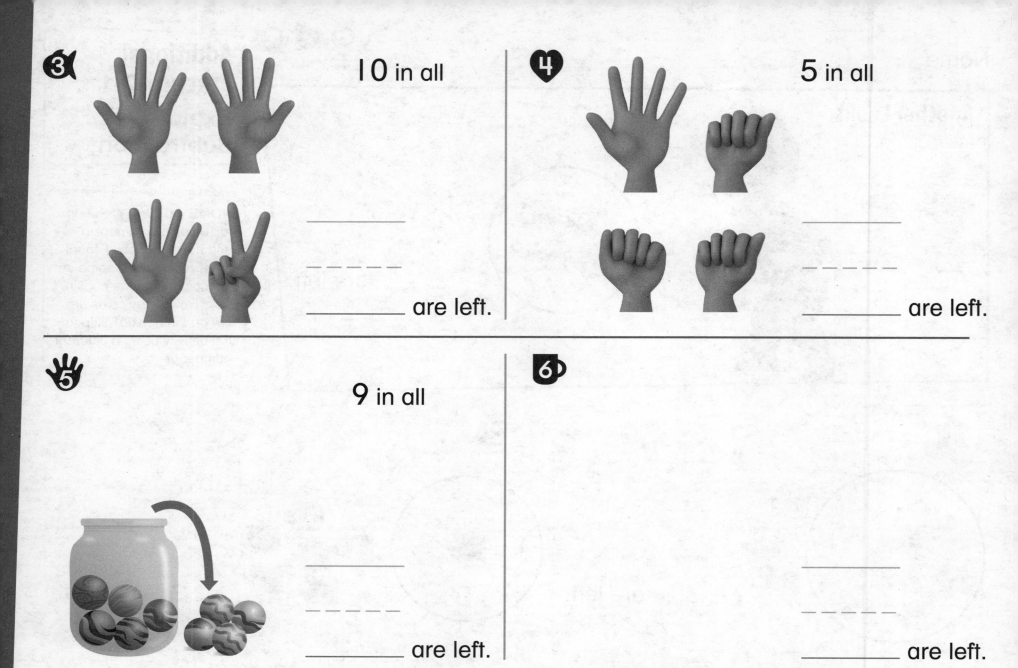

❸ 10 in all

_____
- - - - -
_____ are left.

❹ 5 in all

_____
- - - - -
_____ are left.

❺ 9 in all

_____
- - - - -
_____ are left.

❻

_____
- - - - -
_____ are left.

Directions Have students listen to the story, and then do all of the following to find how many are left: give an explanation of a mental image, use objects to act it out, and hold up fingers. Ask them to write the number to tell how many are left. ❸ _10 fingers are in the air. 3 are put down. How many fingers are left?_ ❹ _5 fingers are in the air. 5 are put down. How many fingers are left?_ ❺ _9 marbles are in a jar. 4 are taken out. How many marbles are left?_ ❻ **Higher Order Thinking** Have students draw 8 marbles. Have them mark Xs on some of them, and then write the number to tell how many marbles are left.

 Topic 7 | Lesson 1

Name _____

Another Look!

Take apart 9.

6 and 3

HOME ACTIVITY Give your child 8 coins. Have him or her use the coins to show a way to take apart 8 into two parts. Then have them write the parts.

 Take apart 6.

_____ and _____

 Take apart 7.

_____ and _____

Directions Say: *Carlos takes apart his cube train. He makes a group of 6 and a group of 3. Draw circles around the cubes to show the parts he made, and then write the numbers to tell the parts.* and Have students take apart each cube train. Have them draw a circle around the parts they made, and then write the numbers to tell the parts.

3

Take apart 8.

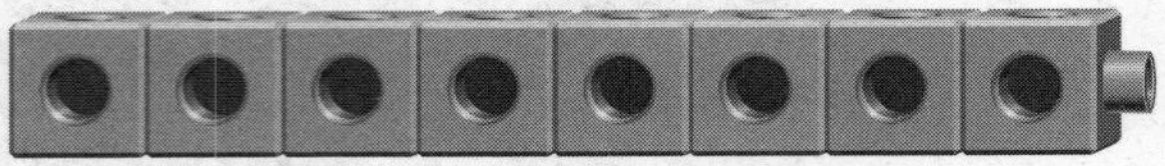

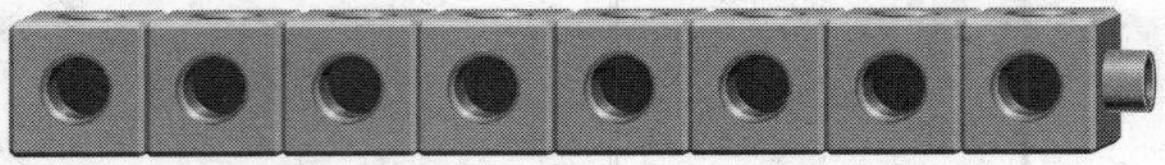

Take apart 8.

_____   and   _____

_____   and   _____

4

_____   and   _____

_____   and   _____

Name _____

Additional Practice 7-3

Represent Subtraction as Taking From

Another Look!

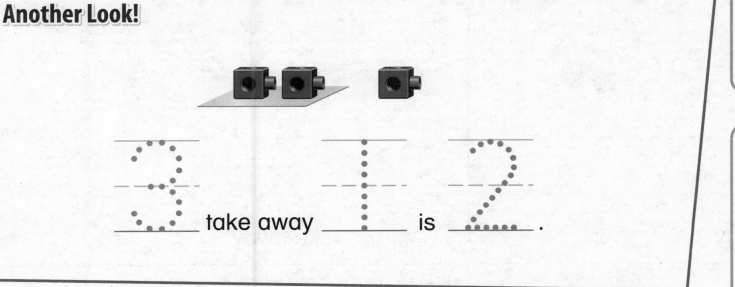

3 take away 1 is 2 .

HOME ACTIVITY Place 7 toys or other small objects in front of your child. Ask him or her to tell you how many toys there are in all, and then move 3 of the toys to the side and tell how many toys are left. Have your child say a sentence that tells how many are left.

1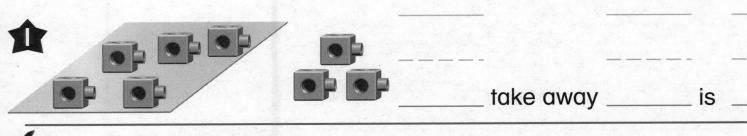

_____ take away _____ is _____ .

2

_____ take away _____ is _____ .

Directions Say: *There are 3 cubes on a mat. Then Alex moves 1 away. How many cubes are left on the mat? Complete the sentence to tell how many are left.* Have students listen to each story, and then complete the sentence to tell how many are left. **1** *Alex puts 8 cubes on a mat. Then he moves 3 away. How many cubes are left on the mat?* **2** *Alex puts 5 cubes on a mat. Then he moves 1 away. How many cubes are left on the mat?*

3

_____ _____ _____ take away _____ is _____ .

4

_____ _____ _____ take away _____ is _____ .

5

_____ _____ _____ take away _____ is _____ .

6

_____ _____ _____ take away _____ is _____ .

Directions Have students listen to each story, count how many are left, and then complete the sentence to tell how many are left. **3** *Carlos sees 6 ducks. 3 fly away. How many ducks are left?* **4** *Carlos sees 6 frogs. 1 hops away. How many frogs are left?* **5 Higher Order Thinking** Have students listen to the story, draw a picture to show what is happening, and then complete the sentence to tell how many are left. *Carlos sees 6 ants. 4 crawl away. How many ants are left?* **6 Higher Order Thinking** Have students listen to the story, draw a picture to show what is happening, and then complete the sentence to tell how many are left. *Some oranges are on Carlos's plate. He eats 2 oranges. 4 are left. How many oranges were on the plate before Carlos ate some?*

Name _____

Another Look!

7 take away 4 is 3.

7 — 4 = 3

HOME ACTIVITY Have your child point to the difference in a number sentence on this page and explain the number. Then give your child 4 toys and help him or her tell a subtracting story. Ask him or her to find the difference. Repeat with other numbers and objects.

⭐ 1

6 take away 4 is 2.

____ ____ ____

____ ____ ____

🍎 2

4 take away 3 is 1.

____ ____ ____

____ ____ ____

Directions Say: *What numbers are being subtracted? Mark Xs on the counters to show how many to take away, and then write the numbers, the minus sign, the equal sign, and the difference to write the equation.* ⭐ and 🍎 Have students mark Xs to show how many counters to take away, and then write an equation to find the difference.

3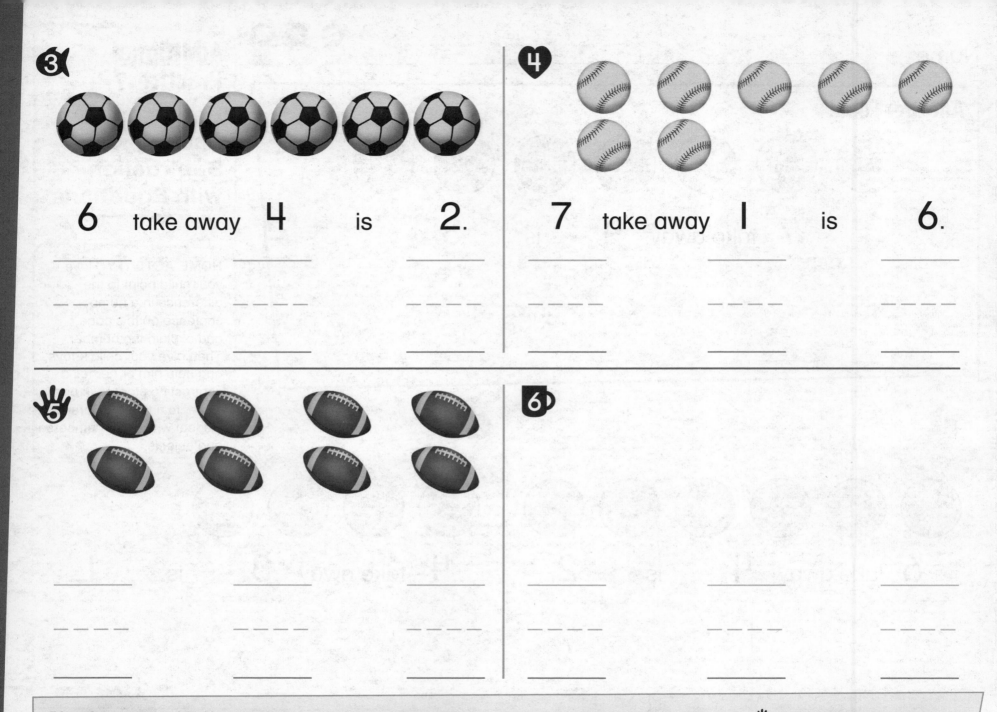

6 take away 4 is 2.

_____   _____   _____

_ _ _ _ _   _ _ _ _ _   _ _ _ _ _

4

7 take away 1 is 6.

_____   _____   _____

_ _ _ _ _   _ _ _ _ _   _ _ _ _ _

5

_____   _____   _____

_ _ _ _ _   _ _ _ _ _   _ _ _ _ _

6

_____   _____   _____

_ _ _ _ _   _ _ _ _ _   _ _ _ _ _

Directions **3** and **4** Have students mark Xs to subtract, and then write an equation to find the difference. **5 Higher Order Thinking** Have students write how many balls there are in all, choose a number to subtract, mark Xs to show how many to take away, and then write the equation to find the difference. **6 Higher Order Thinking** Have students listen to the story, draw counters and mark Xs to show the problem, and then write an equation to find the difference. *Some baseballs are in a bag. 3 are taken out. There are 6 baseballs left.*

Name _____

Another Look!

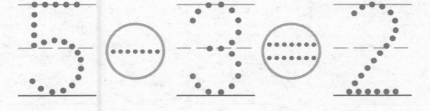

 ①

 ②

HOME ACTIVITY Give your child 7 small objects and ask him or her to give you 3 of the objects. Ask your child to tell you how many objects are left, and ask how he or she knows. Then ask your child to write an equation (7 − 3 = 4).

Directions Say: *There are 5 cubes. 3 are taken away. How many cubes are left? You can draw cubes and mark Xs to show what is happening. Write an equation.* Have students listen to each story, draw pictures to show what is happening, and then write an equation. ① *There are 6 chipmunks. 4 run under a bush. How many chipmunks are left?* ② *There are 5 raccoons. 2 climb up a tree. How many raccoons are left?*

3 ⬢

_____   ⬜   _____   ⬜   _____

4 ♥

_____   ⬜   _____   ⬜   _____

5 ✋

$$6 - 5 = 1$$

6 ☕

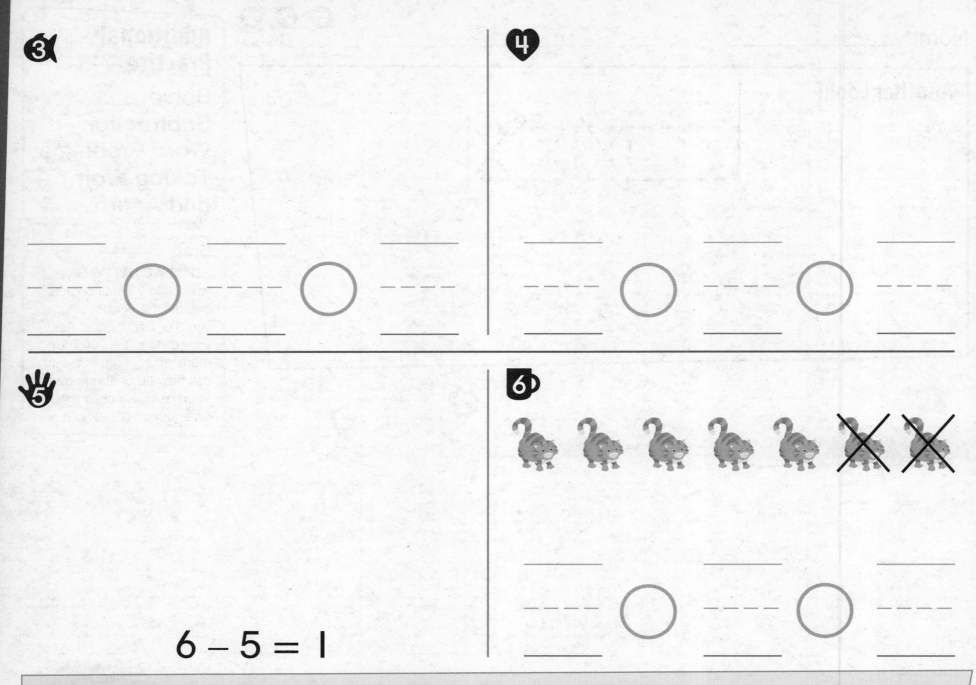

_____   ⬜   _____   ⬜   _____

Directions Have students listen to each story, draw a picture to show what is happening, and then write an equation. **3** *Marta has 9 dog biscuits. She gives her dog 5 of them. How many biscuits are left?* **4** *Marta buys 7 tennis balls. Her brother borrows 4 of them. How many balls are left?* **5 Higher Order Thinking** Have students tell a number story that matches the equation, and then draw a picture to show what is happening. **6 Higher Order Thinking** Have students tell a subtraction story about the cats, and then write an equation.

Topic 7 | Lesson 5

Name _____

Another Look!

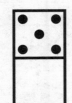 $5 - 0 = 5$

$5 - 1 = 4$

HOME ACTIVITY On a piece of paper, write: $3 - 3 = ?$; $3 - 2 = ?$; $3 - 1 = ?$; $3 - 0 = ?$. Have your child draw pictures for each problem, complete each equation, and then explain the pattern. (0, 1, 2, 3)

 $5 - \underline{\quad} = \underline{\quad}$

 $5 - \underline{\quad} = \underline{\quad}$

 $5 - \underline{\quad} = \underline{\quad}$

 $5 - \underline{\quad} = \underline{\quad}$

Directions Say: *Emily plays with dot tiles. She subtracts the side with fewer dots from the side with more dots. Write the numbers to tell how many dots are on each side, and then write how many are left after she subtracts.* ⭐ Have students use the dot tiles to complete the equations to find the pattern, and then explain the pattern they see.

②
$4 - \underline{} = \underline{}$

$4 - \underline{} = \underline{}$

$4 - \underline{} = \underline{}$

③

$10 - 3 = 7$

$10 - 7 = \underline{}$

④

$5 - 0 = 5$

$5 - \underline{} = 0$

Directions **②** Have students mark Xs to complete the pattern, and then write an equation for each row of flowers. **③ Higher Order Thinking** Have students find the pattern, and then complete the equation. **④ Higher Order Thinking** Have students find the pattern, and then write the missing number in the equation.

92 ninety-two

Topic 7 | Lesson 6

Name _____

Another Look!

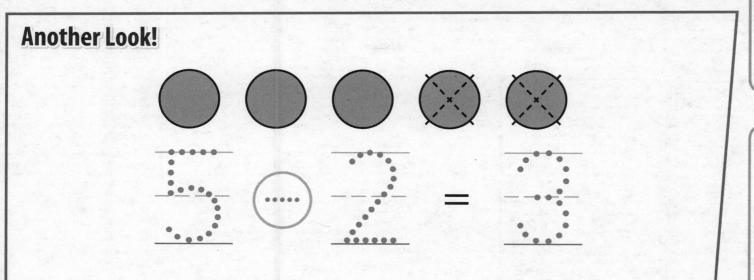

$$5 \underset{\cdots}{\bigcirc} 2 = 3$$

HOME ACTIVITY Give your child 5 spoons and then 2 more spoons. Ask how many there are in all. Have him or her explain whether he or she added or subtracted. Then have your child use the spoons to model the equation.

 1

_____ $\bigcirc$ _____ = _____

 2

_____ $\bigcirc$ _____ = _____

Directions Say: *You can use counters to help you decide whether a story is an addition or subtraction problem. Listen to this story:* Emily built 5 sandcastles. Waves knocked down 2 of them. How many sandcastles are left? *Model this story with counters. Did you add or subtract? Mark Xs on the counters to show subtraction, and then write the equation.* Have students listen to each story, use counters or other objects to help them solve the problem, mark Xs on the counters to show subtraction or draw counters to show addition, and then write the equation. ★ *Emily sees 2 balls at the beach. Later that day, she sees 3 more. How many balls does Emily see in all?* ❷ *Emily has 6 sand shovels. Her brothers lose 3 of them. How many sand shovels are left?*

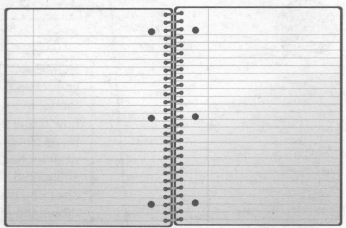

_ _ _ _   ◯   _ _ _ _   =   _ _ _ _

_ _ _ _   _ _ _ _   _ _ _ _

Directions Read the problem aloud. Then have students use multiple problem-solving methods to solve the problem. Say: _Emily has 7 stickers. She gives 2 to her brother. Then she sticks some stickers in her notebook. Emily has 3 stickers left. How many stickers did Emily put in her notebook?_ ✪ **Make Sense** _What are you trying to find out? Will you use addition or subtraction to solve the problem?_ ❹ **Use Tools** _What tool can you use to help solve the problem? Tell a partner and explain why._ ✋ **Be Precise** _Did you write the equation correctly? Explain what the numbers and the symbols mean in the equation._

Name _____

Another Look!

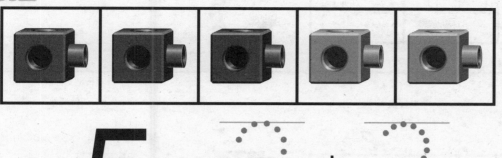

$$5 = 3 + 2$$

HOME ACTIVITY Tell your child you have 4 counters, some are red and some are yellow. Ask your child to draw a picture to show how many red and how many yellow counters you could have. Then complete the equation 4 = __ + __. Repeat using the number 5.

 1

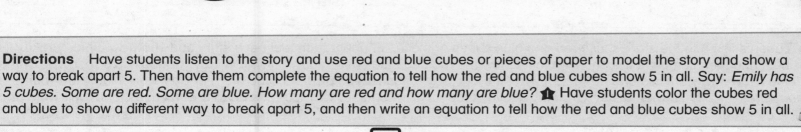

$$5 = \text{------} + \text{------}$$

Directions Have students listen to the story and use red and blue cubes or pieces of paper to model the story and show a way to break apart 5. Then have them complete the equation to tell how the red and blue cubes show 5 in all. Say: *Emily has 5 cubes. Some are red. Some are blue. How many are red and how many are blue?* 1 Have students color the cubes red and blue to show a different way to break apart 5, and then write an equation to tell how the red and blue cubes show 5 in all.

Topic 8 | Lesson 1   Go Online | SavvasRealize.com   ninety-five **95**

2 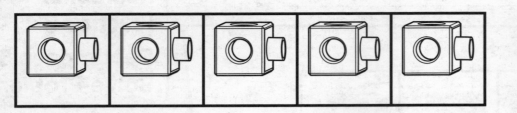 **5** = _____ + _____

---

3 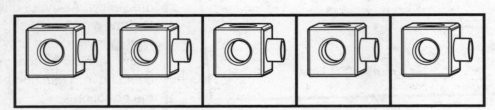 **5** = _____ + _____

4

_____ = _____ + _____

_____   _____   _____

Directions Have students listen to the stories, use red and blue cubes or pieces of paper to model each story and show a way to break apart 5, color the cubes, and then complete the equation to tell how the red and blue cubes show 5 in all. **2** Say: *Carlos has 5 markers. Some are red. Some are blue. How many are red and how many are blue?* **3** Say: *Jada has 5 flowers. Some are red. Some are blue. How many are red and how many are blue?* **4** **Higher Order Thinking** Have students draw another way to break apart 5 with cubes, and then write an equation to match the drawing.

Topic 8 | Lesson 1

Name _____

Additional Practice 8-2
Related Facts

Another Look!

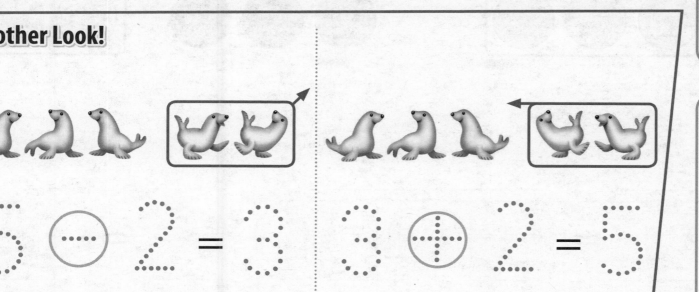

$$5 \odot 2 = 3 \qquad 3 \oplus 2 = 5$$

HOME ACTIVITY Using household objects such as pennies or paper clips, ask your child to make a group of 4 or 5 objects. Then ask your child to break that group into two smaller groups and write an equation about the groups. Then have him or her write an equation to match it, using a different operation.

_____ ◯ _____ = _____

_____ ◯ _____ = _____

Directions Say: *Listen to each story and use counters or other objects to help act out each story to choose an operation. Then complete the equations to tell the related facts. 5 seals are playing. 2 leave. How many seals are left? There are 3 seals playing and 2 join them. How many seals are there in all?* Have students listen to each story, use counters or other objects to help act out the story to choose an operation, and then write the equations to tell the related facts. *4 seals are in a group. 1 walks away. How many seals are left?* Then say: *3 seals are in a group. 1 joins them. How many seals are there in all?*

2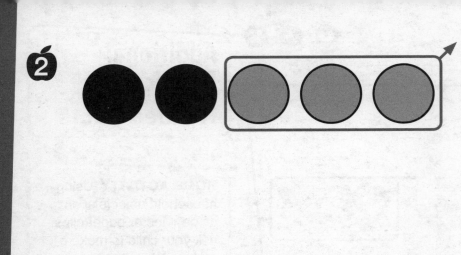

_____   _____
    =   _____
_____

_____   _____
_____   =   _____
_____

3

4

$$4 + 1 = 5$$

$$5 - 1 = 4$$

Directions **2** Have students decide whether the counters show addition or subtraction, and then write equations to tell the related facts. **3** **Higher Order Thinking** Have students draw and color counters to match the equation.
4 **Higher Order Thinking** Have students draw and color counters to match the equation.

 Topic 8 | Lesson 2

Name _____

Additional Practice 8-3
Reasoning

Another Look!

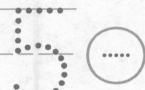 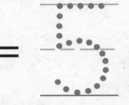

5 ⊙ 0 = 5

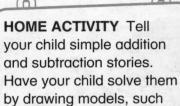
HOME ACTIVITY Tell your child simple addition and subtraction stories. Have your child solve them by drawing models, such as those in the lesson, or by using his or her own representations of the problems.

 ⭐

 ⃝ ＝

Directions Say: *You can use a picture to tell a story for 5 – 0.* Have students use the picture to tell a story, and then write the equation.
⭐ Have students tell a story for 3 – 1. Then have them draw a picture to illustrate their story and write the equation.

Topic 8 | Lesson 3

Go Online | SavvasRealize.com

ninety-nine **99**

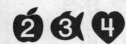

$$3 + 2 = \underline{\quad\quad}$$

Directions Read the problem to students. Then have them use multiple problem-solving methods to solve the problem. Say: *Marta's teacher challenges the class. She asks the class to tell two different stories for one equation:* $3 + 2 = \boxed{}$. *Can you tell two different stories for that equation?* ❷ **Reasoning** *What story can you tell first to help solve the problem and complete the equation?* ❸ **Generalize** *What can you use from your first story to help you tell the second story? What will repeat in the second equation?* ❹ **Use Tools** *Does drawing pictures help to solve the problem? What do your pictures show? What other tools can you use to solve the problem?*

 Topic 8 | Lesson 3

Name _____

Additional Practice 8-4
Fluently Add and Subtract to 5

Another Look!

$1 + 1 = ?$

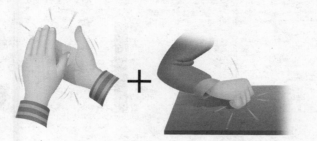

$1 + 1 = \underline{2}$

HOME ACTIVITY Show your child the equation $2 + 3 = ?$. Have him or her solve the problem any way he or she chooses. Then have your child explain how to solve the problem. Repeat for the equation $3 - 3 = ?$.

1 $2 + 2 = \underline{\hspace{1cm}}$

2 $2 - 1 = \underline{\hspace{1cm}}$

3 $0 + 3 = \underline{\hspace{1cm}}$

4 $5 - 4 = \underline{\hspace{1cm}}$

Directions Say: *There are many ways to solve an equation. Try clapping and knocking to solve 1 + 1. Write the number to tell how many in all.*
1–4 Have students solve the equation any way they choose, and then tell how they solved the problem.

5 $5 - 3 = \underline{\hspace{2cm}}$

6 $1 + 3 = \underline{\hspace{2cm}}$

7 $4 - 3 = \underline{\hspace{2cm}}$

8 $5 + 0 = \underline{\hspace{2cm}}$

9 $4 - \underline{\hspace{2cm}} = 2$

10 $\underline{\hspace{2cm}} + 4 = 4$

Directions 👋–**8** Have students solve the equation any way they choose, and then tell how they solved the problem. **9 Higher Order Thinking** Have students solve for the missing number in the equation any way they choose, and then tell how they solved the problem. **10 Higher Order Thinking** Have students solve for the missing number in the equation any way they choose, and then tell how they solved the problem.

Name _____

Additional Practice 8-5
Decompose 6 and 7 to Solve Problems

Another Look!

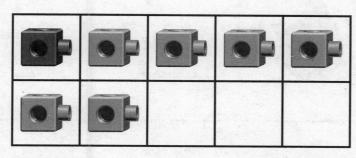

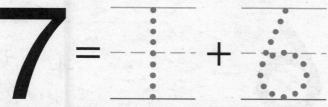

$7 = \underline{} + \underline{}$

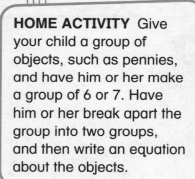

HOME ACTIVITY Give your child a group of objects, such as pennies, and have him or her make a group of 6 or 7. Have him or her break apart the group into two groups, and then write an equation about the objects.

 1

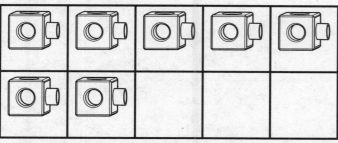

$7 = \underline{\hspace{2cm}} + \underline{\hspace{2cm}}$

 2

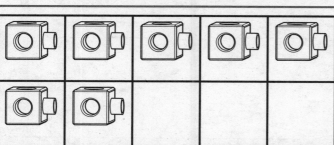

$7 = \underline{\hspace{2cm}} + \underline{\hspace{2cm}}$

Directions Say: *Jada has 7 flowers. She puts some in a red vase and some in a blue vase. How many flowers did she put in each vase?* Have students complete the equation to show one possible way to break apart 7 flowers. **1** and **2** Have students use and color cubes to show 2 other ways the flowers can be put in the vases. Then complete the equation to match each way.

3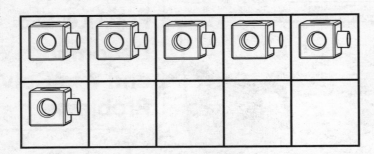

$$6 = \text{\_\_\_\_} + \text{\_\_\_\_}$$

4

$$6 = \text{\_\_\_\_} + \text{\_\_\_\_}$$

5

$$\text{\_\_\_\_} = \text{\_\_\_\_} + \text{\_\_\_\_}$$

Name _____

Another Look!

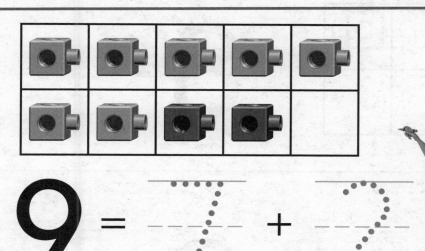

$9 = 7 + 2$

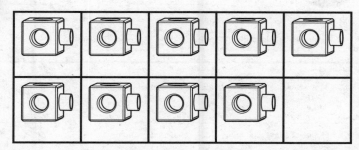

$9 = \underline{\hspace{1cm}} + \underline{\hspace{1cm}}$

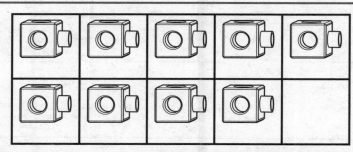

$9 = \underline{\hspace{1cm}} + \underline{\hspace{1cm}}$

Directions Say: *9 students need crayons. Some crayons are blue and some are red. How can you break apart 9 to show how many of each color there will be if each student picks a crayon?* Have students complete the equation to show one possible answer. ★ and ② Have students listen to the story again, use cubes or pieces of paper to model another way to break apart 9 crayons, and color the cubes to tell how many of each color. Then complete the equation to match the cubes.

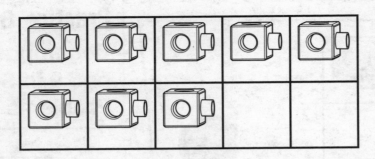

$8 =$ _____ $+$ _____

❤️

$8 =$ _____ $+$ _____

_____ $=$ _____ $+$ _____

Name _____

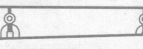
Another Look!

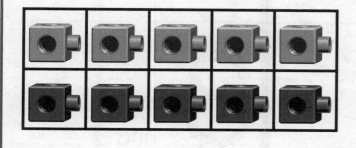

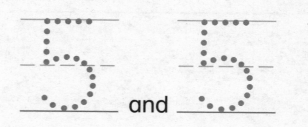

___ and ___

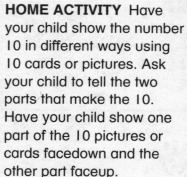
HOME ACTIVITY Have your child show the number 10 in different ways using 10 cards or pictures. Ask your child to tell the two parts that make the 10. Have your child show one part of the 10 pictures or cards facedown and the other part faceup.

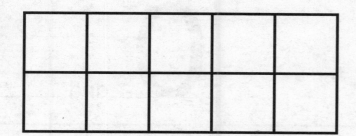

_____   _____

- - - - - - -   - - - - - - -

_____ and _____

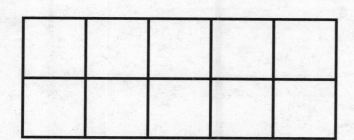

_____   _____

- - - - - - -   - - - - - - -

_____ and _____

Directions Say: *Use red and blue cubes or pieces of paper to model this way to make 10, and then write the numbers.* ⭐ and ❷ **Vocabulary** Have students use red and blue cubes or pieces of paper to find two different ways to make **ten**, draw the cubes to show each way, and then write the numbers.

Topic 8 | Lesson 7   Go Online | SavvasRealize.com   one hundred seven   **107**

3 🪣 🪣 🪣 🪣

4 🧤 🧤 🧤 **3** and _____

5 ✋ **0** and _____

6 ☕

_____ and _____ | _____ and _____

4 _____ and _____

Topic 8 | Lesson 7

Name _____

Another Look!

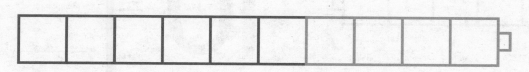

$$10 = 6 + 4$$

HOME ACTIVITY Draw 10 circles. Have your child count the circles. Then have him or her color in some of the circles. Have your child write an equation that tells how many circles are empty and how many are not.

$$10 = \underline{\hspace{1cm}} + \underline{\hspace{1cm}}$$

$$10 = \underline{\hspace{1cm}} + \underline{\hspace{1cm}}$$

Directions Say: *10 students need a raincoat. Some raincoats are red and some are blue. How can you break apart 10 to show how many of each color there will be if each student wears a raincoat?* Have students complete the equation to show one possible answer. ★ and ② Have students listen to the story again, use cubes or pieces of paper to model another way to break apart 10, and color the cubes to tell how many of each color raincoat. Then complete the equation to match the cubes.

③

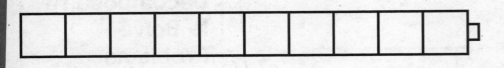

$$10 = \underline{\hspace{1.5cm}} + \underline{\hspace{1.5cm}}$$

④

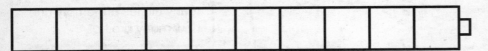

$$\underline{\hspace{1.5cm}} = \underline{\hspace{1.5cm}} + \underline{\hspace{1.5cm}}$$

✋5

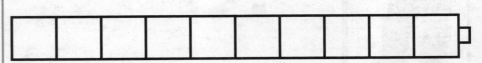

$$10 = 7 + 3$$

$$\underline{\hspace{1.5cm}} = \underline{\hspace{1.5cm}} + \underline{\hspace{1.5cm}}$$

Directions ③ Have students listen to the story again, use and color cubes to show how to break apart 10 a different way to tell how many of each color raincoat. Then complete the equation to match their answer. ④ **Number Sense** Have students color the cube train red and yellow to show two different parts that add to 10, and then write an equation to match the number pair. ✋ **Higher Order Thinking** Have students color the cube train red and yellow to match the equation, and then write a different equation to match the cube train. Have students tell how the equations are both alike and different.

 Topic 8 | Lesson 8

Name _____

Another Look!

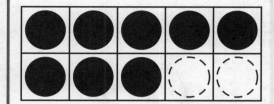

$$8 + 2 = 10$$

HOME ACTIVITY Hold up your hands in front of your child with 1 index finger straight and the rest of your fingers bent. Ask your child to tell you the parts of 10 that your fingers show (1 and 9). Then ask your child to write an equation for those parts of 10 (1 + 9 = 10). Repeat the activity with different combinations of straight and bent fingers.

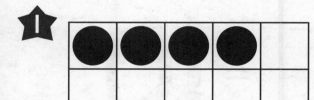

$$4 + \underline{\quad} = 10$$

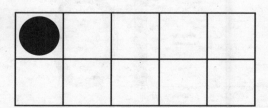

$$1 + \underline{\quad} = 10$$

Directions Say: *You can show parts of 10 with counters and a ten-frame. Draw the missing part of 10, and then write the missing number in the equation to tell the parts of 10.* ⭐ and ❷ Have students count the counters to find one part of 10, draw counters to show the other part, and then write the missing number in the equation to tell the parts of 10.

③ 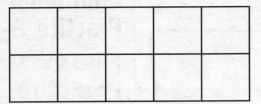 $5 + \text{------} = 10$

④ 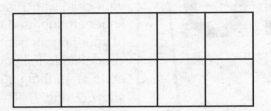 $7 + \text{------} = 10$

✋5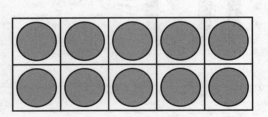

$\text{------} + \text{------} = 10$

$\text{------} + \text{------} = 10$

112 one hundred twelve

Topic 8 | Lesson 9

Name _____

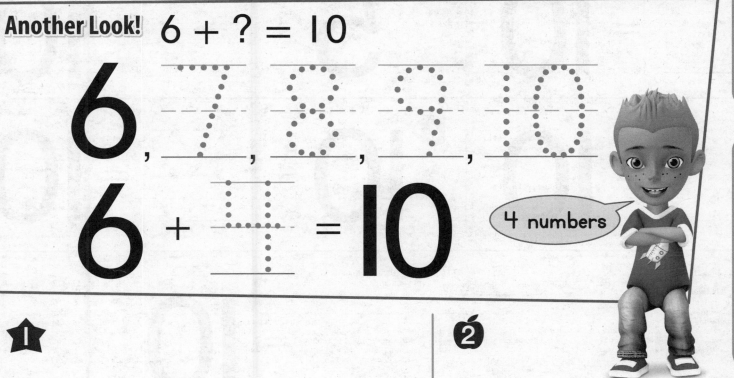

Another Look! $6 + ? = 10$

6, 7, 8, 9, 10

$6 + 4 = 10$

4 numbers

HOME ACTIVITY Give your child 7 small objects such as coins or beans. Ask your child to add objects until he or she has 10 objects. Then have your child fill in the missing number in this equation: $7 + ? = 10$ (3). Repeat the activity by starting with groups of 5, 8, and 9 objects.

★ 1

❷

$9 + \underline{\quad} = 10$ $2 + \underline{\quad} = 10$

Directions Say: *You can count on to find the missing part of 10. Count on from 6 until you reach 10. How many numbers did you count? Write the missing number in the equation.* ★–❷ Have students show how to count on to find the missing part of 10, and then write the missing number in the equation. Then have them explain how they know their answer is correct.

3 $7 + \underline{\hspace{2cm}} = 10$

4 $5 + \underline{\hspace{2cm}} = 10$

5 $1 + \underline{\hspace{2cm}} = 10$

6 $10 + \underline{\hspace{2cm}} = 10$

7 $\underline{\hspace{2cm}} + \underline{\hspace{2cm}} = 10$

8 $\underline{\hspace{2cm}} + \underline{\hspace{2cm}} = \underline{\hspace{2cm}}$

Directions **3**–**6** Have students count on to find the missing part of 10, and then write the missing number in the equation. Then have them tell how they know their answer is correct. **7 Algebra** Say: *Roxy borrowed 10 colored pencils from Hannah. When she returned them, there were only 8 colored pencils in the box. How many colored pencils were missing?* Have students write the missing numbers in the equation, and then tell how they know their answers are correct. **8 Higher Order Thinking** Have students draw counters to find the missing part of 10, and then write the equation to match the counters.

Name _____

Another Look!

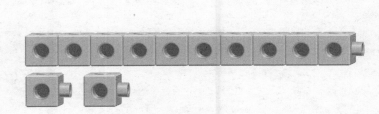

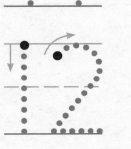

HOME ACTIVITY Draw groups of 11 and 12 circles, each on a separate index card. Have your child write the correct number on the back of each card. Then use the cards to practice counting and writing the numbers 11 and 12.

 ★ 1

 🍎 2

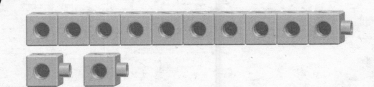

Directions Say: *Count the connecting cubes, and then write the number to tell how many.* ⭐ and ❷ Have students count the connecting cubes, and then write the number to tell how many.

3

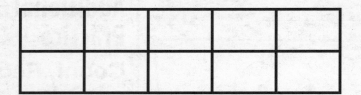

_____

- - - - - - - - - - - - - -

_____

4

_____

- - - - - - - - - - - - - -

_____

5

_____

- - - - - - - - - - - - - -

_____

Directions ❸ Have students use the ten-frame to show 11 yo-yos, and then practice writing the number that tells how many. ❹ **Higher Order Thinking** Have students draw 12 toys, and then practice writing the number that tells how many. ✋ **Higher Order Thinking** Have students count each group of cars, and then write the numbers to tell how many.

Name _____

Another Look!

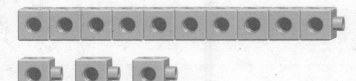

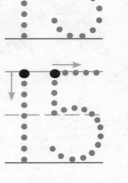

Additional Practice 9-2

Count, Read, and Write 13, 14, and 15

HOME ACTIVITY Have your child write the numbers 13, 14, and 15 on 3 index cards. Show your child groups of 13, 14, and 15 objects. Have her or him count the objects in each group, say the numbers, and match the number cards to the groups.

_____

_ _ _ _ _ _ _

_____

_____

_ _ _ _ _ _ _

_____

Directions Say: *Count the connecting cubes, and then write the number to tell how many.* 🌟 and ❷ Have students count the connecting cubes, and then write the number to tell how many.

3

4

5

118 one hundred eighteen   Copyright © Savvas Learning Company LLC. All Rights Reserved.   **Topic 9 | Lesson 2**

Name _____

Another Look!

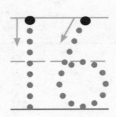

HOME ACTIVITY Have your child write the numbers 16 and 17 on 2 index cards. Show your child groups of 16 and 17 objects. Have him or her count the objects, say the numbers, and match the number cards to the groups.

_____

- - - - - - - - -

_____

2

_____

- - - - - - - - -

_____

Directions Say: *Count the connecting cubes, and then write the number to tell how many.* **1** and **2** Have students count the connecting cubes, and then write the number to tell how many.

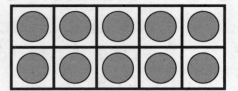

_____

_ _ _ _ _ _ _ _ _

❹

_____

_ _ _ _ _ _ _ _ _

❺

_____   _____

_ _ _ _ _ _ _ _   _ _ _ _ _ _ _ _

Directions ❸ Have students count the counters showing the number of cat toys, and then practice writing the number that tells how many. ❹ **Higher Order Thinking** Have students draw 16 balls, and then practice writing the number that tells how many. ❺ **Higher Order Thinking** Have students count each group of piggy banks, and then write the numbers to tell how many.

Name _____

Another Look!

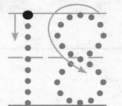

HOME ACTIVITY Have your child draw 18 objects, and then write the number 18 below the group of objects. Repeat for the numbers 19 and 20.

_____

- - - - - - - -

_____

_____

- - - - - - - -

_____

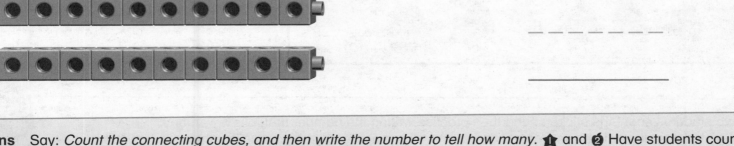

Directions Say: *Count the connecting cubes, and then write the number to tell how many.* ★ and ② Have students count the connecting cubes, and then write the number to tell how many.

3

_____

- - - - - - - - - - - - - -

_____

4

_____

- - - - - - - - - - - - - -

_____

5

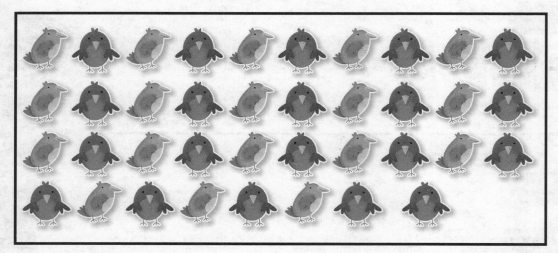

_____   _____

- - - - - - - -   - - - - - - - -

_____   _____

122 one hundred twenty-two

Topic 9 | Lesson 4

Name _____

Another Look!

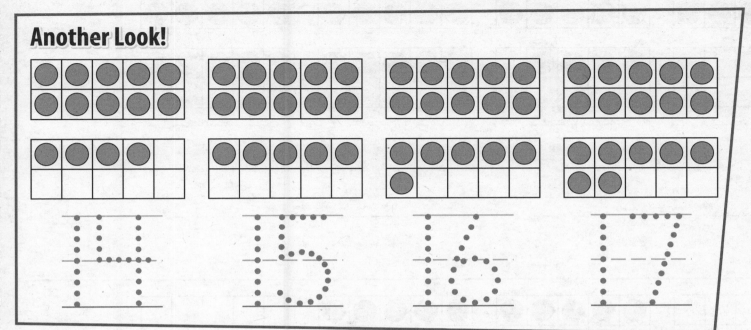

HOME ACTIVITY Pick a start number between 1 and 15. Have your child write the next four numbers. Repeat using different numbers.

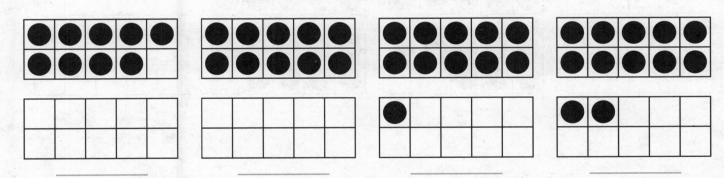

Directions Say: *The first double ten-frame shows 14 counters. The second double ten-frame shows 1 more counter. Count the counters in each double ten-frame, and then write the numbers to tell how many. Count forward to say each number you wrote.* ⭐ Have students count the counters in each double ten-frame, and then write the numbers to tell how many. Then have them count forward to say each number they wrote.

2

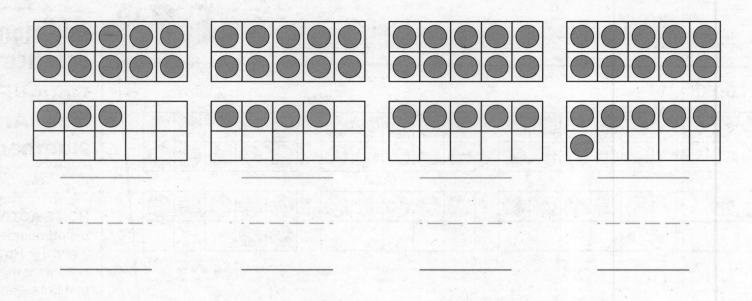

_____ _____ _____ _____

3

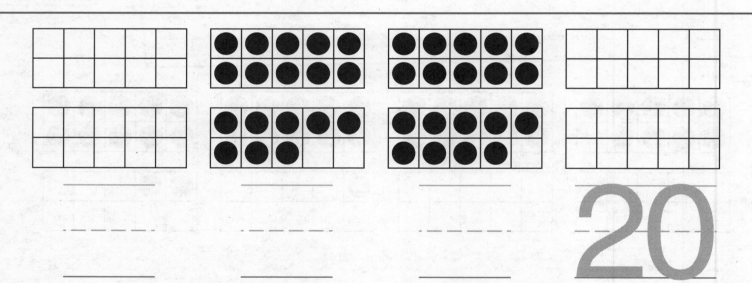

_____ _____ _____ **20**

_____

Name _____

 Video Tools Games

Another Look!

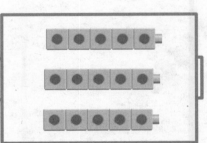

HOME ACTIVITY Give your child a handful of small items such as pennies, buttons, or dry beans. Have him or her count how many of each item there are. Count together to check your child's answers. Then line up the same number of objects in another arrangement. Have him or her count to see that the number is the same.

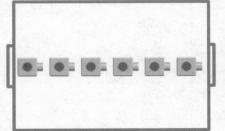

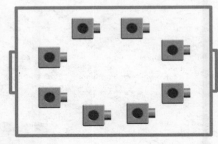

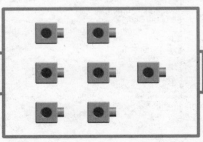

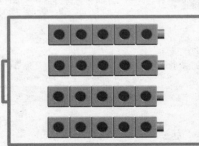

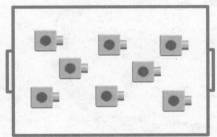

Directions Say: *Which trays have 20 connecting cubes on them? Draw a circle around the trays. How did you find how many?* Have students: ⭐ draw a circle around the tray with 8 cubes; ❷ draw a circle around the tray with 7 cubes.

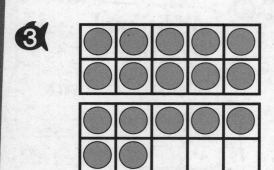 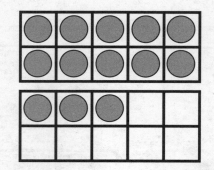 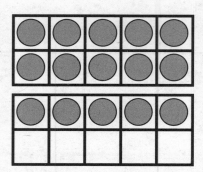

4

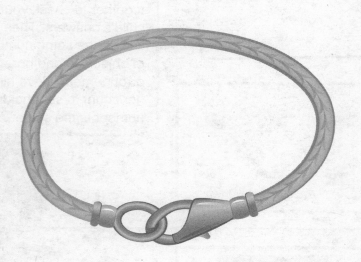

5

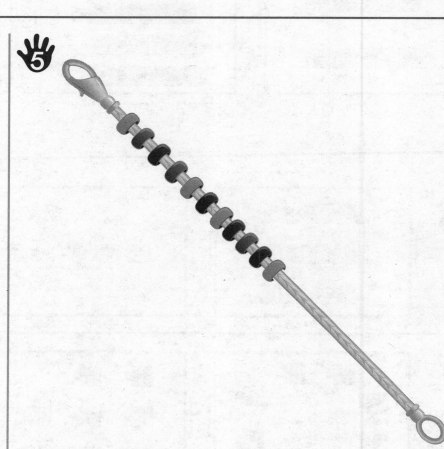

Directions ❸ Have students draw a circle around the double ten-frame with 17 counters. **4 Higher Order Thinking** Have students draw 11 beads on the bracelet. ✋ **Higher Order Thinking** Have students draw more beads to show 20 beads on the bracelet.

Name _____

Another Look!

13 14 15 16 (17) (18)

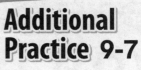

HOME ACTIVITY Put 15 coins on a table. Say: *I have some coins on the table. I am hiding 1 or more coins in my hand. How many coins could I have in all? 13, 14, 15, 16, or 17?* Have your child count the coins on the table and then explain how he or she knows how many coins there could be in all.

16 17 18 19 20

10 11 12 13 14

Directions Say: *There are 1 or more counters inside the jar. Count the counters, and then draw a circle around the numbers that tell how many counters there could be in all.* ⭐ and ② Say: *There are 1 or more counters inside the jar. Count the counters, and then draw a circle around the numbers that tell how many counters there could be in all.*

Directions Read the problem to students. Then have them use multiple problem-solving methods to solve the problem. Say: *Jada knows that there are 17 bunnies at the animal sanctuary. Some are sitting in the grass. Some are hiding behind a bush. What clues can she write to have her friends guess the number of bunnies in all?* ❸ **Make Sense** *What do you know about the problem? How many bunnies are there in all?* ❹ **Reasoning** *Tell your friend the clues. How many bunnies can he or she see?* ✋ **Explain** *If your friend says there are 14 bunnies in all, what mistake did he or she probably make?*

 Topic 9 | Lesson 7

Name _____

Another Look!

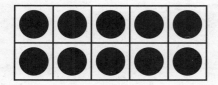
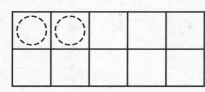

 + 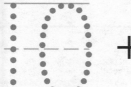 =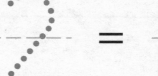

HOME ACTIVITY Have your child use pennies to model and explain how to make 11, 12, and 13 with 10 ones and some more ones.

 ⭐

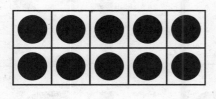

_____   _____   _____

_ _ _ _ + _ _ _ _ = _ _ _ _

_____   _____   _____

Directions Say: *You can use counters and a double ten-frame to show 12 as 10 ones and some more ones. Fill the first ten-frame with 10 counters. Then draw more counters to make 12, and write an equation to match the picture.* ⭐ Have students draw counters to make 13 and write an equation to match the picture. Then have them tell how the picture and equation show 10 ones and some more ones.

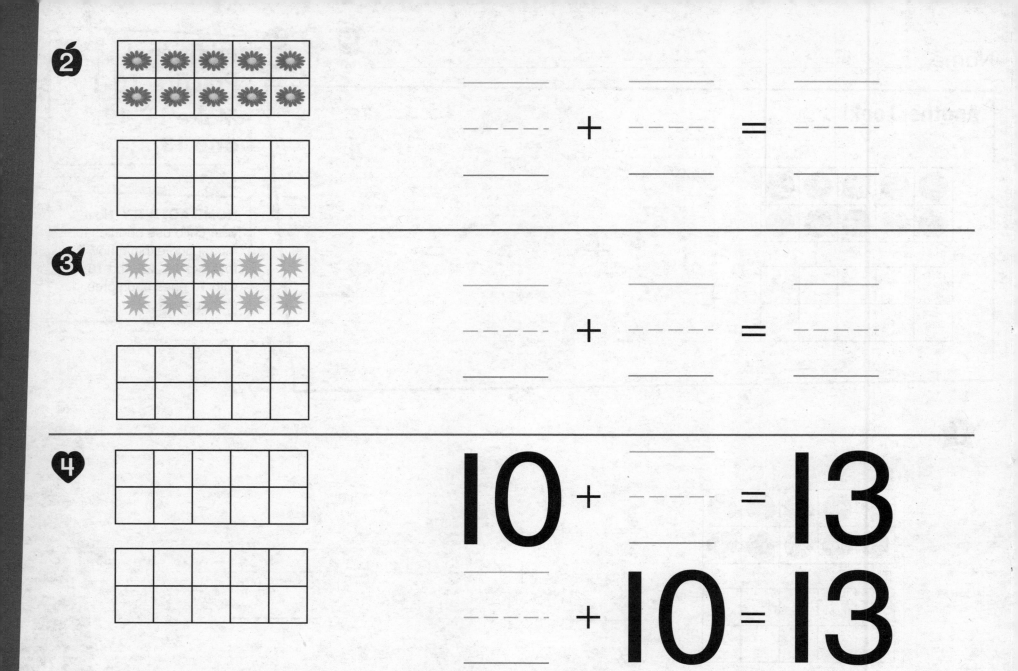

2 _____ _____ + _____ _____ = _____ _____

     _____ + _____ = _____

3 _____ _____ + _____ _____ = _____ _____

     _____ + _____ = _____

4 10 + _____ = 13

     _____ + 10 = 13

Name _____

Another Look!

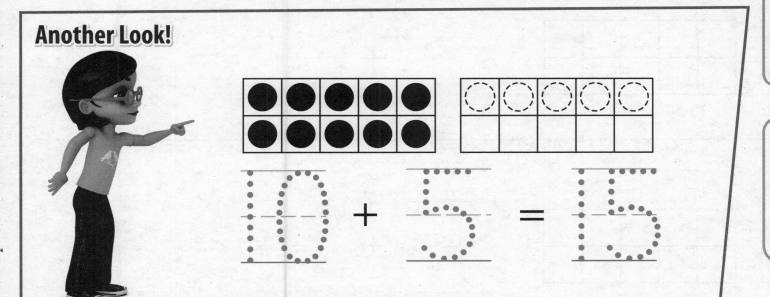

HOME ACTIVITY Have your child model the number 14 by drawing a big circle with 10 Xs inside the circle and 4 Xs outside the circle. Repeat with the numbers 15 and 16.

$$10 + 5 = 15$$

 ⭐  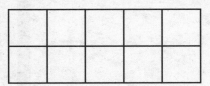   _ _ _ _ _ + _ _ _ _ _ = _ _ _ _ _

 ❷ 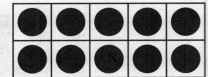 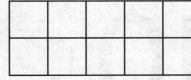   _ _ _ _ _ + _ _ _ _ _ = _ _ _ _ _

Directions Say: *Finish drawing counters in the ten-frame to make 15. Then write an equation to match the picture. The picture and equation show one way to make 15 with 10 ones and some more ones.* Have students: ⭐ draw counters to make 14, and write an equation to match the picture. Then have them tell how the picture and equation show 10 ones and some more ones; ❷ draw counters to make 16 and write an equation to match the picture. Then have them tell how the picture and equation show 10 ones and some more ones.

_____ + _____ = _____

4

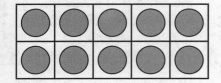   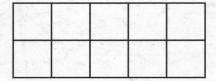

_____ + _____ = _____

5

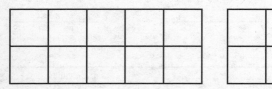   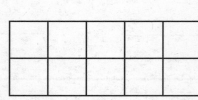

$10 + \_\_\_\_ = 14$

$\_\_\_\_ + 10 = 14$

Directions Have students: **3** draw counters to show how to make 15 and write an equation to match the picture. Then have them tell how the picture and equation show 10 ones and some more ones; **4** draw counters to show how to make 16 and write an equation to match the picture. Then have them tell how the picture and equation show 10 ones and some more ones. **5 Higher Order Thinking** Have students draw counters to find the missing numbers in the equations. Then have them tell how the picture and equations show 10 ones and some more ones.

   Topic 10 | Lesson 2

Name _____

Another Look!

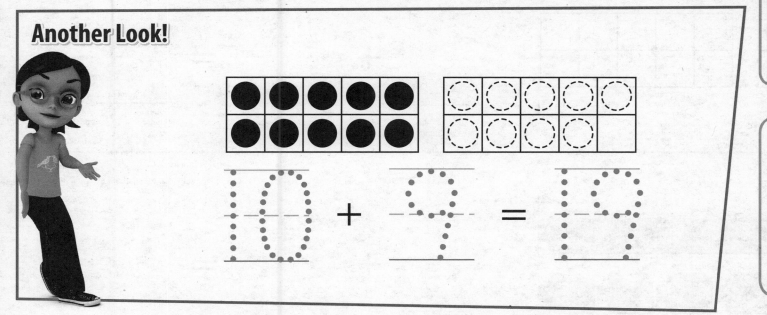

10 + 9 = 19

HOME ACTIVITY Place 10 marbles or other small objects in a bowl. In a second bowl, have your child count on from 10 while adding objects until there are 17 objects in all. Repeat with 19 and then 18 objects in all.

⭐ 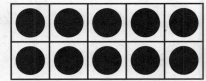 _____ + _____ = _____

🍎 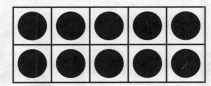 _____ + _____ = _____

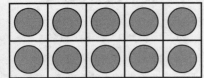   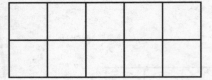

_____ + _____ = _____

_____   _____   _____

4

_____ + _____ = _____

_____   _____   _____

5

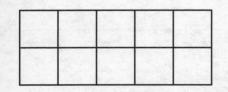

$18 = 10 + \underline{\quad}$

$10 + \underline{\quad} = 18$

Directions Have students: **3** draw counters to make 19, and then write an equation to match the picture. Then have them tell how the picture and equation show 10 ones and some more ones; **4** look at the cubes showing 17, and then write an equation to match the picture. Then have them tell how the picture and equation show 10 ones and some more ones. ✋ **Higher Order Thinking** Have students draw counters to find the missing numbers in the equations. Then have them tell how the picture and equation show 10 ones and some more ones.

     Topic 10 | **Lesson 3**

Video   Tools   Games

Another Look!

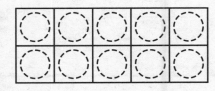

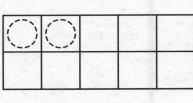

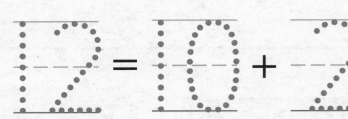

$$12 = 10 + 2$$

HOME ACTIVITY Have your child sort a group of 12 pencils into one group of 10 pencils and one group of 2 pencils. Discuss how many pencils are in each group and how many pencils there are in all. Repeat with 13 pencils and 11 pencils.

$$\underline{\hspace{2cm}} = \underline{\hspace{2cm}} + \underline{\hspace{2cm}}$$

Directions Say: *Draw counters in the double ten-frame to show 12 and write an equation to match the picture. The picture and equation show 10 ones and some more ones.* ⭐ Have students draw counters to show 11 and write an equation to match the picture. Then have them tell how the picture and equation show 10 ones and some more ones.

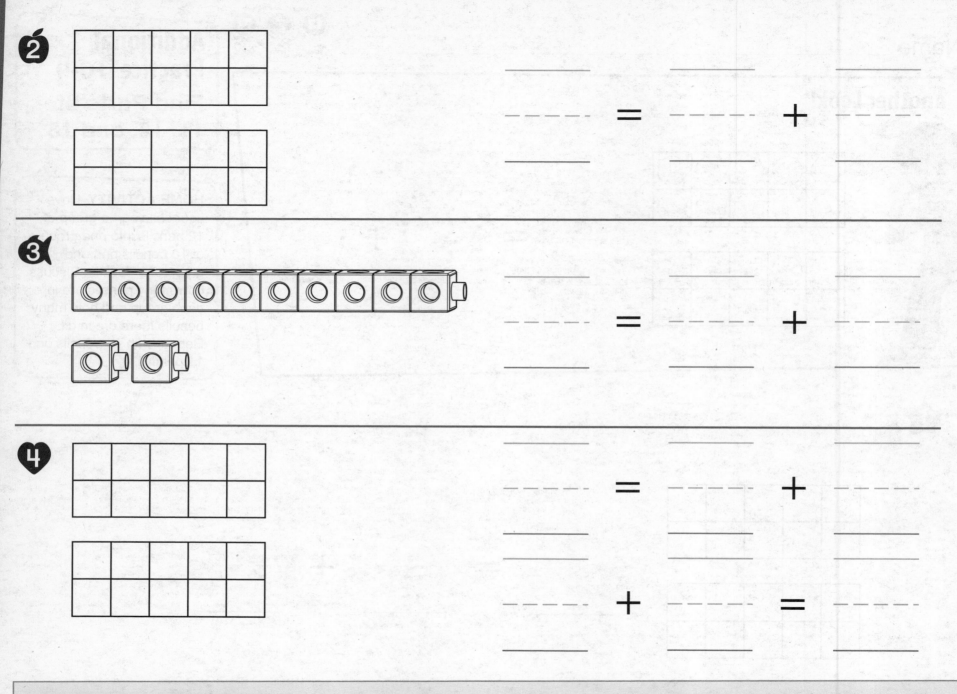

2

_____ = _____ + _____

3

_____ = _____ + _____

4

_____ = _____ + _____

_____ + _____ = _____

Copyright © Savvas Learning Company LLC. All Rights Reserved.

Name _____

Another Look!

$$15 = 10 + 5$$

HOME ACTIVITY Draw 14 boxes, and then shade 10 of them. Have your child tell how many boxes there are in all. Then have your child tell how many boxes are shaded and how many boxes are NOT shaded. Repeat with 16 boxes and 15 boxes.

1

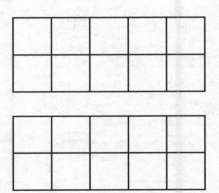

$$14 = \underline{\hspace{1.5cm}} + \underline{\hspace{1.5cm}}$$

Directions Say: *Draw counters in the double ten-frame to show 15 and complete the equation to match the picture. The picture and equation show 10 ones and some more ones.* ★ Have students draw counters to show 14 and complete the equation to match the picture. Then have them tell how the picture and equation show 10 ones and some more ones.

2

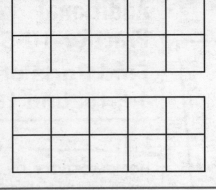

$$16 = \text{-----} \quad + \quad \text{-----}$$

3

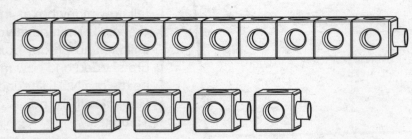

$$15 = \text{-----} \quad + \quad \text{-----}$$

4

$$\text{-----} = \text{-----} \quad + \quad \text{-----}$$

$$\text{-----} + \text{-----} = \text{-----}$$

Directions Have students: **2** draw counters to show 16 and complete the equation to match the picture. Then have them tell how the picture and equation show 10 ones and some more ones; **3** color the cubes blue and red to show 15 and complete the equation to match the picture. Then have them tell how the picture and equation show 10 ones and some more ones. **4 Higher Order Thinking** Have students draw counters to show 14 and write two equations to match the picture. Then have them tell how the picture and equations show 10 ones and some more ones.

138 one hundred thirty-eight

Topic 10 | Lesson 5

Name _____

Additional Practice 10-6
Find Parts of 17, 18, and 19

Another Look!

$$18 = 10 + 8$$

HOME ACTIVITY Have your child sort a group of 18 objects into a group of 10 and a group of 8. Discuss how many objects there are in each group and how many there are in all. Repeat with 17 objects and 19 objects.

$$17 = \underline{} + \underline{}$$

Directions Say: *Draw counters to show 18, and then complete the equation to match. How do the picture and equation show 10 ones and some more ones?* ★ Have students draw counters to show 17, and then complete the equation to match the picture. Then have them tell how the picture and equation show 10 ones and some more ones.

2

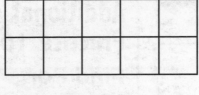

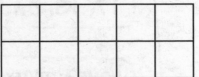

$19 = \underline{\hspace{2cm}} + \underline{\hspace{2cm}}$

3

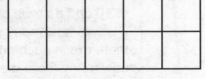

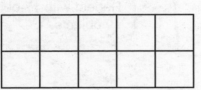

$18 = \underline{\hspace{2cm}} + \underline{\hspace{2cm}}$

4

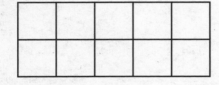

$\underline{\hspace{2cm}} = \underline{\hspace{2cm}} + \underline{\hspace{2cm}}$

$\underline{\hspace{2cm}} + \underline{\hspace{2cm}} = \underline{\hspace{2cm}}$

Directions Have students: **2** draw counters to show 19, and then complete the equation to match the picture. Then have them tell how the picture and equation show 10 ones and some more ones; **3** draw counters to show 18, and then complete the equation to match the picture. Then have them tell how the picture and equation show 10 ones and some more ones. **4 Higher Order Thinking** draw counters to show 17, and then write two equations to match the picture. Then have them tell how the picture and equations show 10 ones and some more ones.

Name _____

Another Look!

9

19

$10 + 9 = 19$

HOME ACTIVITY Take 11 pennies or other small household objects and arrange them in the following manner: two rows of 5 pennies, and a single penny underneath. Have your child write the equation that describes the number of pennies $(10 + 1 = 11)$. Repeat for quantities of 12 pennies, 13 pennies, and so on, up to 19 pennies. Have your child explain the pattern in the equations that he or she has written.

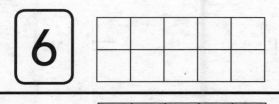

6

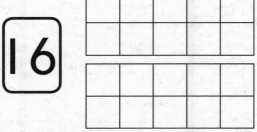

16

_____ _____ _____

_ _ _ _ _ + _ _ _ _ _ = _ _ _ _ _

Directions Say: *Read the numbers on the cards, and then draw counters in the top ten-frame to show 9 and in the bottom ten-frames to show 19. Write an equation to match the drawings in the ten-frames. Tell how the picture and the equation show 10 ones and some more ones.* ⭐ Have students read the numbers on the cards, and then draw counters in both the top and bottom ten-frames to show how many. Then have them write an equation to match the drawings in the ten-frames. Have students tell how the picture and the equation show 10 ones and some more ones.

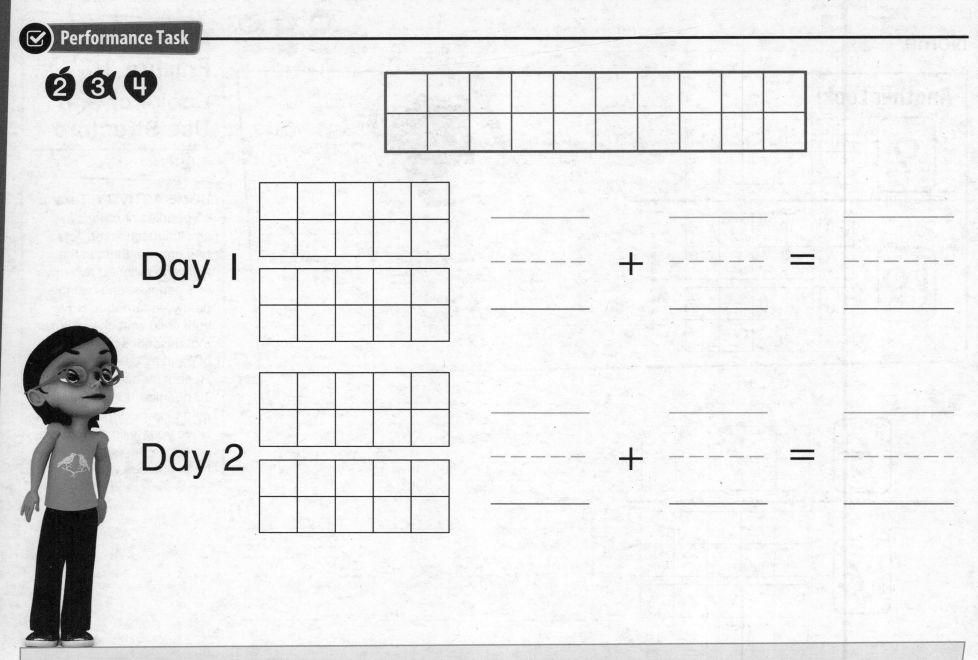

Day 1

Day 2

_____ + _____ = _____

_____ + _____ = _____

Directions Read the problem to students. Then have them use multiple problem-solving methods to solve the problem. Say: *Alex got a new tablet computer. It came loaded with 10 apps. Every day, Alex is allowed to upload 1 more app. How many apps will Alex have in two days?* ❷ **Model** *Can a model help you solve the problem? Write the numbers in the number chart. Which numbers will help solve this problem?* ❸ **Use Tools** *How can you use the ten-frames to help? Draw counters to show how many apps there will be on Alex's tablet for each day. Then write equations to help you see the pattern.* ❹ **Use Structure** *How many apps will Alex have in three days? How did seeing a pattern help you solve the problem? Explain your answer.*

Name _____

Another Look!

1	2	3	4	5	6	7	8	9	10
11	12	13	14	15	16	17	18	19	20
21	22	23	24	25	26	27	28	29	30

HOME ACTIVITY Tell your child a number between 1 and 10. Ask him or her to count up to 30 from that number.

 1

1	2	3	4	5	6	7	8	9	10
11	12	13	14	15	16	17	18	19	20
21	22	23	24	25	26	27	28	29	30

2

Directions Say: *Listen to these numbers, and then draw a circle around the numbers in the chart that you hear: nine, nineteen, twenty-nine. What number do you see in each box of the column? What number do you hear in each number?* Have students listen to the numbers, and then draw a circle around the numbers in the chart that they hear: ★ *four, fourteen, twenty-four;* ② *sixteen, seventeen, eighteen, nineteen.*

3

1	2	3	4	5	6	7	8	9	10
11	12	13	14	15	16	17	18	19	20
21	22	23	24	25	26	27	28	29	30

4

5

1	2	3	4	5	6	7	8	9	10
11	12	13	14	15	16	17	18	19	20
21	22	23	24	25	26	27	28	29	30

6

Directions Have students: **3** point to the numbers in the shaded column, say them aloud, and then explain how the numbers in that column are alike; **4** listen to the numbers, and then draw a circle around the numbers in the chart that they hear: *twenty-seven, twenty-eight, twenty-nine, thirty;* **5** listen to the numbers, and then draw a circle around the numbers in the chart that they hear: *twenty, twenty-one, twenty-two, twenty-three.* **6** **Higher Order Thinking** Have students count aloud the numbers in the middle row. Say: *Do you hear the number "one" in eleven? What other numbers that you counted are like the number 11? Color these numbers and explain how they are alike.*

Name _____

Another Look!

1	2	3	4	5	6	7	8	9	10
11	12	13	14	15	16	17	18	19	20
21	22	23	24	25	26	27	28	29	30
31	32	33	34	35	36	37	38	39	40
41	42	43	44	45	46	47	48	49	50

HOME ACTIVITY Tell your child a number under 50. Ask him or her to count from that number up to 50. Repeat with different numbers.

1	2	3	4	5	6	7	8	9	10
11	12	13	14	15	16	17	18	19	20
21	22	23	24	25	26	27	28	29	30
31	32	33	34	35	36	37	38	39	40
41	42	43	44	45	46	47	48	49	50

Directions Have students point to the fourth row. Say: *Listen to the following numbers, and then draw a circle around the numbers in the chart that you hear:* thirty-three, thirty-four, thirty-five, thirty-six, thirty-seven. *What number do you see in almost every box of this row? What number do you hear in those numbers?* Have students listen to the numbers, draw a circle around the numbers in the chart that they hear, and then tell what is repeated in each number: ⭐ *twenty-six, twenty-seven, twenty-eight, twenty-nine;* ❷ *forty-one, forty-two, forty-three, forty-four.*

1	2	3	4	5					10
11	12	13	14	15	16	17	18	19	20
21	22	23	24	25	26	27	28	29	30
31	32	33	34	35	36	37	38	39	40
41	42	43	44	45	46	47	48	49	50

1	2	3	4	5	6	7	8	9	10
11	12	13	14	15	16	17	18	19	20
21	22	23	24	25	26	27	28	29	30
31	32	33	34	35	36	37	38	39	40
41	42	43	44	45	46	47	48	49	50

Directions Have students: 🐟 say the missing numbers in the top row aloud as they count forward from 5 to 10, and then explain how they know they are correct; 💙 look at the circled numbers in the top row. Then have students look at the numbers that are circled in the rows below. Ask: *What pattern do you see?* Have students draw circles to complete the pattern for the other numbers in the chart. ✋ **Higher Order Thinking** Have students listen to the numbers, and then color the numbers they hear in the chart: *ten, twenty, thirty, forty, fifty.*

Video Tools Games

Another Look!

1	2	3	4	5	6	7	8	9	10
11	12	13	14	15	16	17	18	19	20
21	22	23	24	25	26	27	28	29	30
31	32	33	34	35	36	37	38	39	40
41	42	43	44	45	46	47	48	49	50
51	52	53	54	55	56	57	58	59	60
61	62	63	64	65	66	67	68	69	70
71	72	73	74	75	76	77	78	79	80
81	82	83	84	85	86	87	88	89	90
91	92	93	94	95	96	97	98	99	100

HOME ACTIVITY Arrange 30 objects, such as pennies, beads, or other small objects, in groups of 10 on a table. Ask your child to use decade numbers to count the number of objects aloud. Repeat with up to 10 groups of objects.

1	2	3	4	5	6	7	8	9	10
11	12	13	14	15	16	17	18	19	20
21	22	23	24	25	26	27	28	29	30
31	32	33	34	35	36	37	38	39	40
41	42	43	44	45	46	47	48	49	50
51	52	53	54	55	56	57	58	59	60
61	62	63	64	65	66	67	68	69	70
71	72	73	74	75	76	77	78	79	80
81	82	83	84	85	86	87	88	89	90
91	92	93	94	95	96	97	98	99	100

Directions Say: *Color green the boxes of the following decade numbers:* ten, forty, fifty, sixty, ninety. ⭐ Have students color orange the boxes of the following decade numbers: *twenty, thirty, fifty, seventy, eighty, one hundred.*

2

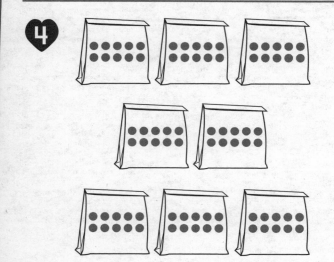

50

60

70

3

80

90

100

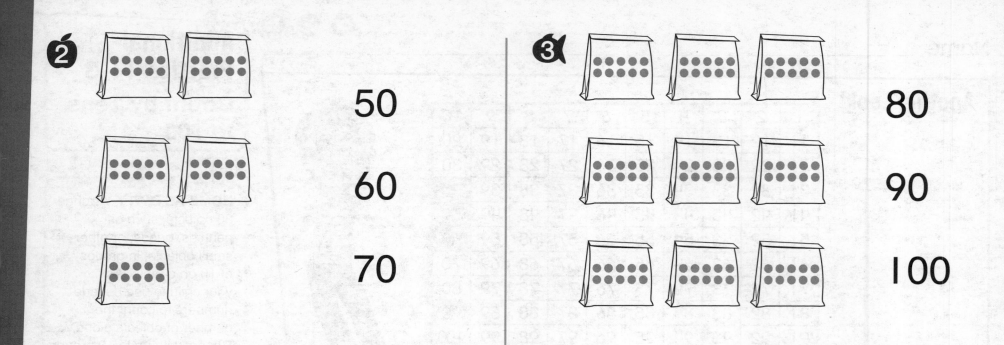

4

1	2	3	4	5	6	7	8	9	10
11	12	13	14	15	16	17	18	19	20
21	22	23	24	25	26	27	28	29	30
31	32	33	34	35	36	37	38	39	40
41	42	43	44	45	46	47	48	49	50
51	52	53	54	55	56	57	58	59	60
61	62	63	64	65	66	67	68	69	70
71	72	73	74	75	76	77	78	79	80
81	82	83	84	85	86	87	88	89	90
91	92	93	94	95	96	97	98	99	100

Directions ❷ and ❸ Have students count the dots, and then draw a circle around the number that tells how many. ❹ **Higher Order Thinking** Have students count the number of dots, and then circle the number in the chart to tell how many. Then have students count forward from the number by tens to 100 and circle the numbers they count.

Name _____

Additional Practice 11-4
Count by Ones to 100

Another Look!

1	2	3	4	5	6	7	8	9	10
11	12	13	14	15	16	17	18	19	20
21	22	23	24	25	26	27	28	29	30
31	32	33	34	35	36	37	38	39	40
41	42	43	44	45	46	47	48	49	50
51	52	53	54	55	56	57	58	59	60
61	62	63	64	65	66	67	68	69	70
71	72	73	74	75	76	77	78	79	80
81	82	83	84	85	86	87	88	89	90
91	92	93	94	95	96	97	98	99	100

HOME ACTIVITY Point to a number on a hundred chart, such as 27. Have your child count from that number to another number you have chosen. Repeat with other numbers.

 1

1	2	3	4	5	6	7	8	9	10
11	12	13	14	15	16	17	18	19	20
21	22	23	24	25	26	27	28	29	30
31	32	33	34	35	36	37	38	39	40
41	42	43	44	45	46	47	48	49	50
51	52	53	54	55	56	57	58	59	60
61	62	63	64	65	66	67	68	69	70
71	72	73	74	75	76	77	78	79	80
81	82	83	84	85	86	87	88	89	90
91	92	93	94	95	96	97	98	99	100

 2

1	2	3	4	5	6	7	8	9	10
11	12	13	14	15	16	17	18	19	20
21	22	23	24	25	26	27	28	29	30
31	32	33	34	35	36	37	38	39	40
41	42	43	44	45	46	47	48	49	50
51	52	53	54	55	56	57	58	59	60
61	62	63	64	65	66	67	68	69	70
71	72	73	74	75	76	77	78	79	80
81	82	83	84	85	86	87	88	89	90
91	92	93	94	95	96	97	98	99	100

Directions Say: *You can count forward from any number. Find and draw a circle around the number* eighteen. *Count aloud until you reach the shaded box. Color the boxes of the numbers you counted aloud.* Have students draw a circle around the given number, and then color the boxes of the numbers as they count aloud, starting at the circled number and ending at the shaded box. Have them: **1** draw a circle around the number *eighty*; **2** draw a circle around the number *thirty-six.*

3

1	2	3	4	5	6	7	8	9	10
11	12	13	14	15	16	17	18	19	20
21	22	23	24	25	26	27	28	29	30
31	32	33	34	35	36	37	38	39	40
41	42	43	44	45	46	47	48	49	50
51	52	53	54	55	56	57	58	59	60
61	62	63	64	65	66	67	68	69	70
71	72	73	74	75	76	77	78	79	80
81	82	83	84	85	86	87	88	89	90
91	92	93	94	95	96	97	98	99	100

4

1	2	3	4	5	6	7	8	9	10
11	12	13	14	15	16	17	18	19	20
21	22	23	24	25	26	27	28	29	30
31	32	33	34	35	36	37	38	39	40
41	42	43	44	45	46	47	48	49	50
51	52	53	54	55	56	57	58	59	60
61	62	63	64	65	66	67	68	69	70
71	72	73	74	75	76	77	78	79	80
81	82	83	84	85	86	87	88	89	90
91	92	93	94	95	96	97	98	99	100

5

1	2	3	4	5	6	7	8	9	10
11	12	13	14	15	16	17	18	19	20
21	22	23	24	25	26	27	28	29	30
31	32	33	34	35	36	37	38	39	40
41	42	43	44	45	46	47	48	49	50
51	52	53	54	55	56	57	58	59	60
61	62	63	64	65	66	67	68	69	70
71	72	73	74	75	76	77	78	79	80
81	82	83	84	85	86	87	88	89	90
91	92	93	94	95	96	97	98	99	100

6

1	2	3	4	5	6	7	8	9	10
11	12	13	14	15	16	17	18	19	20
21	22	23	24	25	26	27	28	29	30
31	32	33	34	35	36	37	38	39	40
41	42	43	44	45	46	47	48	49	50
51	52	53	54	55	56	57	58	59	60
61	62	63	64	65	66	67	68	69	70
71	72	73	74	75	76	77	78	79	80
81	82	83	84	85	86	87	88	89	90
91	92	93	94	95	96	97	98	99	100

Directions Have students draw a circle around the given number, and then color the boxes of the numbers as they count aloud, starting at the circled number and ending at the shaded box. Have them: **3** draw a circle around the number *twenty-two*; **4** draw a circle around the number *fifty-one*. **5** **Higher Order Thinking** Have students draw a circle around the number that comes after *sixteen*, the number that comes after *forty-eight*, and the number that comes after *eighty*. **6** **Higher Order Thinking** Have students listen to the count, and then color the boxes of the missing numbers: 67, 68, 69, 70, 72, 73, 74, 76.

Topic 11 | Lesson 4

Video Tools Games

Another Look!

1	2	3	4	5	6	7	8	9	10
11	12	13	14	15	16	17	18	19	20
21	22	23	24	25	26	27	28	29	30
31	32	33	34	35	36	37	38	39	40
41	42	43	44	45	46	47	48	49	50

HOME ACTIVITY Point to a hundred chart from this lesson. Take turns making up riddles and guessing the answers. For example, ask your child: *What number comes just after 31 and just before 33?* (32)

1

1	2	3	4	5	6	7	8	9	10
11	12	13	14	15	16	17	18	19	20
21	22	23	24	25	26	27	28	29	30
31	32	33	34	35	36	37	38	39	40
41	42	43	44	45	46	47	48	49	50

2

1	2	3	4	5	6	7	8	9	10
11	12	13	14	15	16	17	18	19	20
21	22	23	24	25	26	27	28	29	30
31	32	33	34	35	36	37	38	39	40
41	42	43	44	45	46	47	48	49	50
51	52	53	54	55	56	57	58	59	60

Directions Say: *Draw a circle around the column with the numbers:* seven, seventeen, twenty-seven, thirty-seven, forty-seven. *What pattern do you see and hear?* Have students: **1** draw a circle around the column that has the number 9 in the top row, count the numbers in this column aloud, and then explain the pattern they see and hear; **2** draw a circle around the number 30 and around the numbers 31 to 39, count the numbers aloud, and then explain the pattern they see and hear.

61	62	63	64	65	66	67	68	69	70
71	72	73	74	75	76	77	78	79	80
81	82	83	84	85	86	87	88	89	90
91	92	93	94	95	96	97	98	99	100

Directions Read the problem aloud. Then have students use multiple problem-solving methods to solve the problem. Say: *Start at 62 and count up 15 squares in any way you choose. Use your yellow crayon and make a path to show how you counted, and then draw a circle around the number where you ended.* **Be Precise** *How many tens are in 15?* **Use Structure** *How does using a number chart help you count forward?* **Generalize** *What number would you end on if you start at 80 and count up 12 squares? Would there be a different way to count that would solve the problem?*

Name _____

Additional Practice 12-1

Two-Dimensional (2-D) and Three-Dimensional (3-D) Shapes

Another Look!

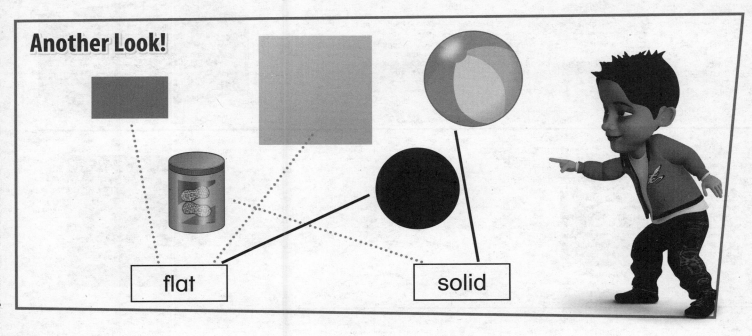

flat

solid

HOME ACTIVITY Point to various objects throughout your house. Have your child tell whether the object is flat or solid. Then have him or her draw a flat shape and a solid object that can be found in the kitchen.

Directions Say: *The black circle is flat. What other objects are flat? Draw a line from the objects that are flat to the box labeled* flat. *The beach ball is solid. Draw a line from other objects that are solid to the box labeled* solid. ⭐ Have students draw a circle around the objects that are flat, and then mark an X on the objects that are solid.

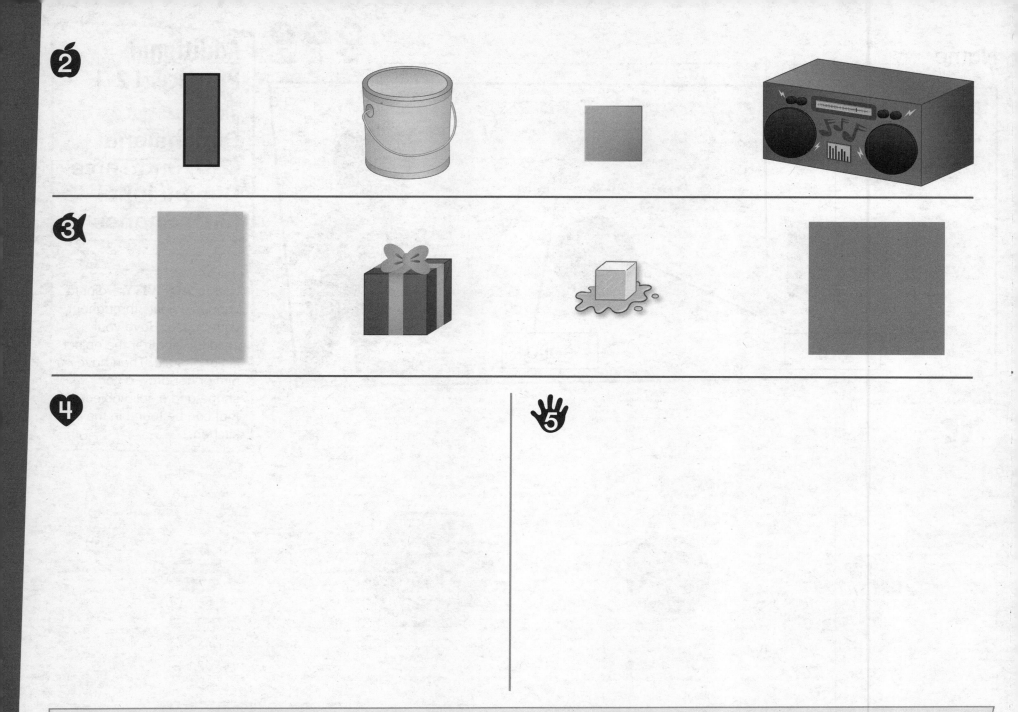

2

3

4

5

Name _____

Additional Practice 12-2
Circles and Triangles

Another Look!

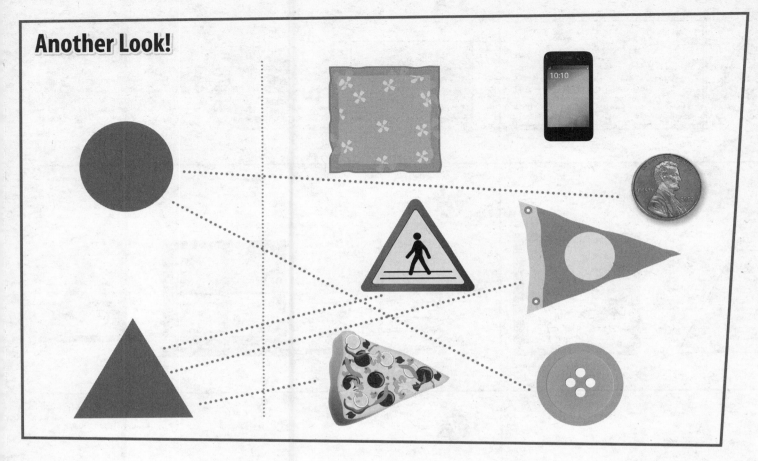

⭐1

Directions Say: *A circle is round. Draw a line from the objects that look like a circle to the gray circle on the left. A triangle has 3 sides and 3 vertices. Draw a line from the objects that look like a triangle to the gray triangle on the left.* ⭐ *Have students draw a box around the objects that look like a triangle and mark an X on the objects that look like a circle.*

2

3

4

5

6

7

Topic 12 | Lesson 2

Name _____

Another Look!

HOME ACTIVITY Take a walk around your home or neighborhood. Ask your child to look for windows that have the shape of a rectangle or a square.

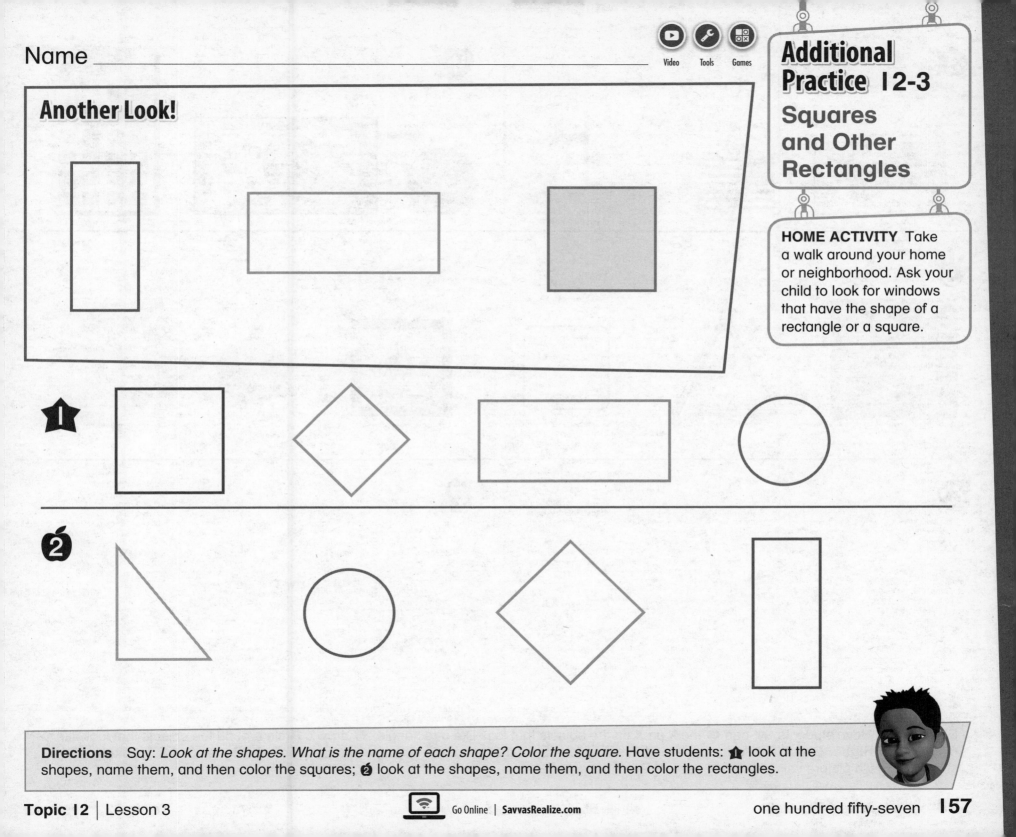

⭐

🍎

Directions Say: *Look at the shapes. What is the name of each shape? Color the square.* Have students: ⭐ look at the shapes, name them, and then color the squares; 🍎 look at the shapes, name them, and then color the rectangles.

3

 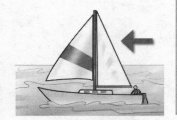

 4

5

  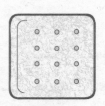   

 6

 7

Directions Have students: **3** and **4** mark an X on the objects that look like a rectangle; **5** draw a circle around the objects that look like a square. **6** **Higher Order Thinking** Have students draw an object that is both a rectangle and a square. **7** **Higher Order Thinking** Have students draw a picture using at least 2 rectangles and 2 squares.

158 one hundred fifty-eight

Topic 12 | Lesson 3

Name _____

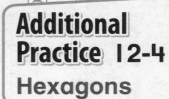

Another Look!

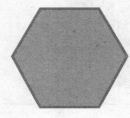 

HOME ACTIVITY Have your child look through newspapers and magazines to identify pictures of objects that look like a hexagon. Then have them draw an object shaped like a hexagon.

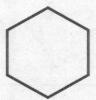 ⭐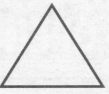

 🍎

Directions Say: *Look at the shapes. What is the name of each shape? Color the hexagons.* ⭐ and 🍎 Have students color the hexagons in each row.

Directions ❸ and ❹ Have students draw a circle around the objects that look like a hexagon. ✋ **Higher Order Thinking** Have students draw a picture of an object that is shaped like a hexagon.

Name _____

Another Look!

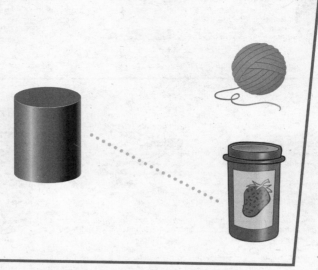

HOME ACTIVITY Show your child several objects that look like cubes, cylinders, spheres, or cones. Ask him or her to name the solid figure that it looks like. For example, show your child a ball and ask him or her to name the shape (sphere).

1

2

Directions Have students point to the cone. Say: *This solid figure is a cone. Draw a line from the cone to the object that looks like that shape. Draw a line from the cylinder to the object that looks like that shape.* Have students: **1** and **2** draw a line from each solid figure to the object that looks like that shape.

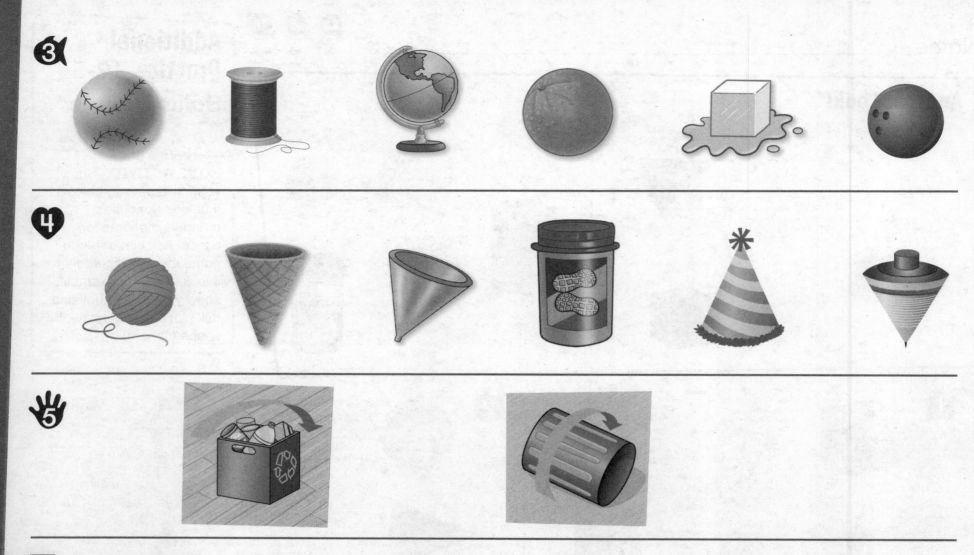

3

4

5

6

Directions **3** and **4** Have students draw a circle around the 4 objects in each row that look like the same shape, and then name the shape. **enVision® STEM** Say: *Pushing on an object can make it move. Some shapes are easier to push than others.* Have students draw a circle around the object that is easier to push. **6** **Higher Order Thinking** Have students draw 2 objects that do NOT look like a sphere. Tell a partner what shapes the objects look like.

Topic 12 | **Lesson 5**

Name _____

Another Look!

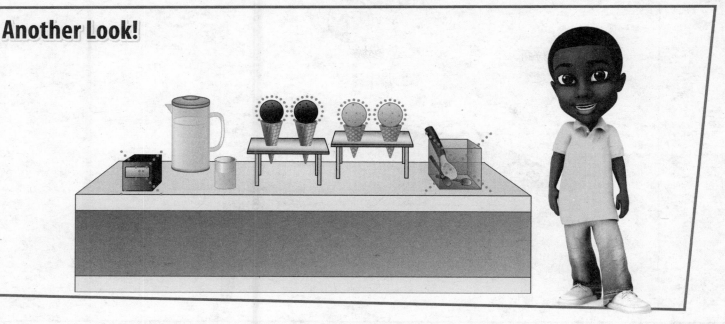

HOME ACTIVITY Have your child identify and name objects in your house that look like a circle, square, rectangle, triangle, hexagon, sphere, cube, cylinder, and cone. Have them tell where each object is located in the house.

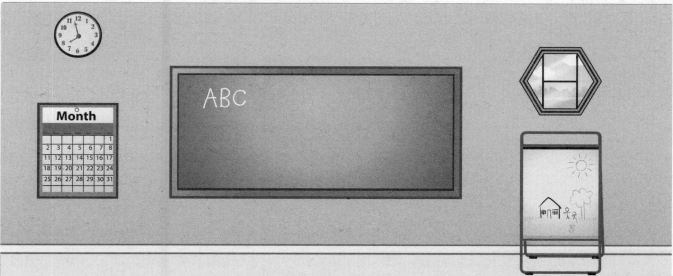

Directions Say: *Point to a scoop of ice cream. What shape is the scoop of ice cream? Find other objects in the picture that look like a sphere and draw a circle around them. Can you find an object that looks like a cube? Mark an X on the objects that look like a cube.*
⭐ Have students point to objects in the picture and name each shape. Then have them draw a circle around the objects that look like a rectangle, and then mark an X on the object that looks like a hexagon.

2

3

Name _____

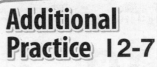

Additional Practice 12-7
Precision

Another Look!

HOME ACTIVITY Place several items on a table, such as a plate, spoon, fork, cup, and napkin. Have your child tell the position of each object using the following words: *above, below, beside, next to, in front of,* and *behind*. For example, a child might say, "The spoon is beside the plate."

1

Directions Say: *Look at the objects in the picture. Name the shapes of the objects you see. Name the object above the basketball. Mark an X on that object. Draw a circle around the object that is next to the basketball and below the block.* ⭐ Have students mark an X on the object that looks like a sphere below the picnic table. Then have them draw a circle around the object that looks like a cylinder beside the tree.

Directions Read the problem to students. Then have them use multiple problem-solving methods to solve the problem. Say: *Marta wants to tell a friend about different things in the kitchen and where they are located. What words can she use?* ❷ **Be Precise** *Mark an X on the object that looks like a cylinder that is behind the object that looks like a cone. What words helped you find the correct object?* ❸ **Reason** *The ice cream cone is next to the sugar cube. What is another way to explain where the ice cream cone is?* ❹ **Explain** *Marta describes the door as looking like a rectangle. She also says it is below the clock. Do you agree or disagree? Explain how you know you are correct.*

Name _____

Another Look!

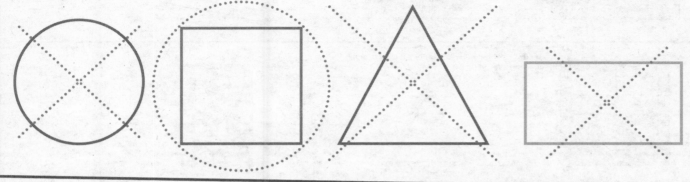

HOME ACTIVITY Play *What Object Am I?* with your child. Think of an object in the house, such as a window or a door, and give clues about it. For example: "I have 4 sides and 4 vertices. All of my sides are the same length. What shape am I?" Then have your child give you clues about an object.

 1

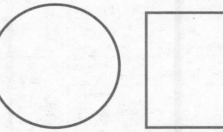

 2

  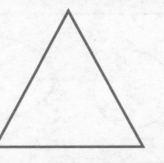 

Directions Say: *Listen to the clues. After each clue, mark an X on any shape that does NOT fit the clue. I have 4 sides. I am a special kind of rectangle because all of my sides are the same length. Draw a circle around the shape that fits all of the clues.* Have students listen to the clues, mark an X on the shapes that do NOT fit the clues, draw a circle around the shape that the clues describe, and then tell how the shapes they marked with an X are similar to the shape they drew a circle around. **1** *I do NOT have 4 vertices. I have 3 sides. What shape am I?* **2** *I have 4 vertices. My sides are NOT all the same length. What shape am I?*

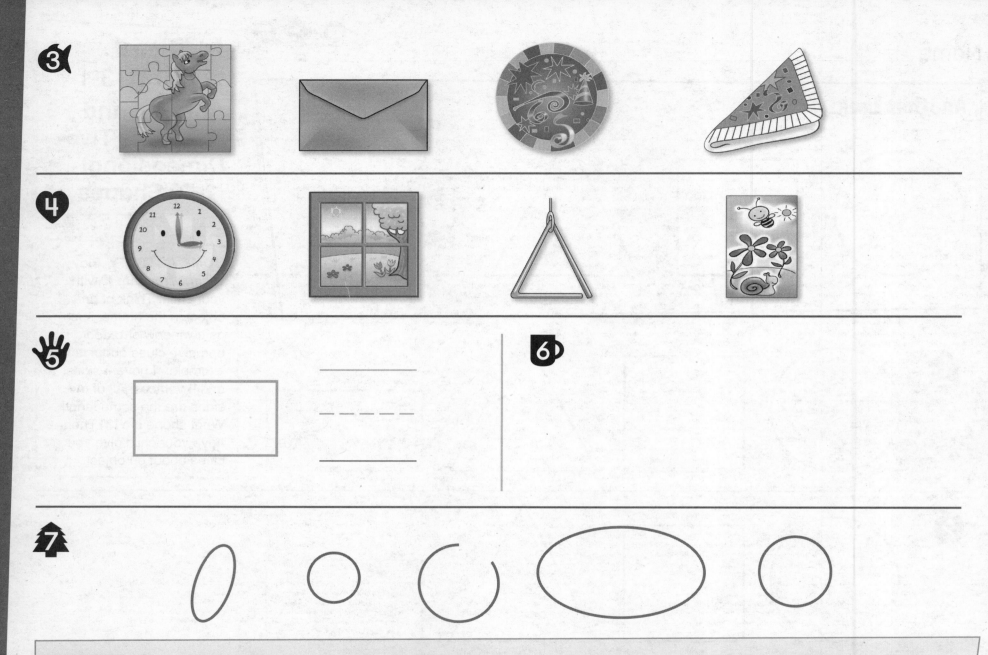

3

4

5

6

7

Name _____

Another Look!

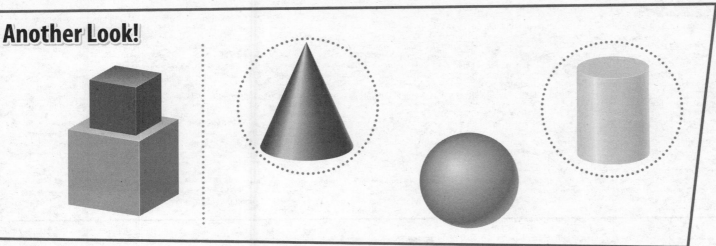

HOME ACTIVITY Show your child a ball, a can, and a cube-shaped block. Ask him or her to compare the features of each object, such as which objects can stack, which can roll, and which can slide. Have your child point to the flat surfaces on each of the objects.

1

2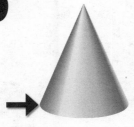

Directions Say: *A cube can stack on top of another cube. Draw a circle around the other solid figures that can also be stacked on top of a cube.* Have students: **1** look at the solid figure on the left that can roll, and then draw a circle around the other solid figures that can roll; **2** look at the solid figure on the left that can slide, and then draw a circle around the other solid figures that can slide.

3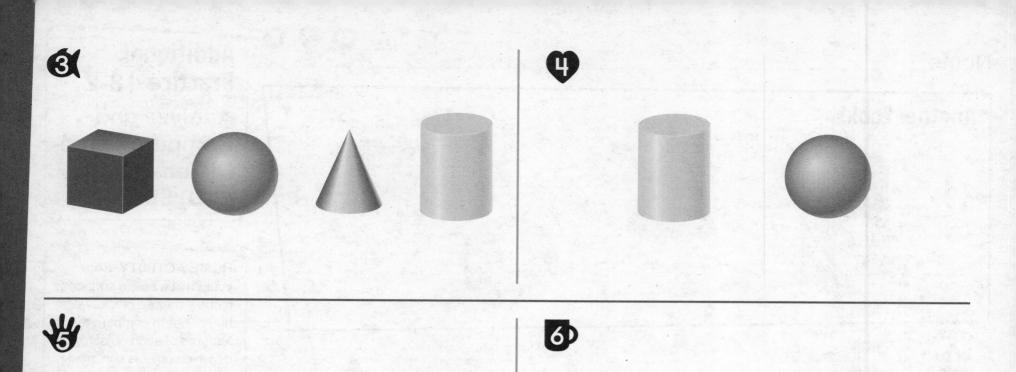

4

5

6

Directions Have students: **3** mark an X on the solid figures that can both roll and slide; **4** mark an X on the solid figure that is NOT a sphere, and then explain how it is similar to and different from a sphere. **5** **Higher Order Thinking** Have students draw 2 solid figures that can roll. **6** **Higher Order Thinking** Have students use all of the 3 solid figures that can stack to draw a castle made of blocks. Then have them explain why cones can only stack on top of other shapes.

Name _____

Another Look!

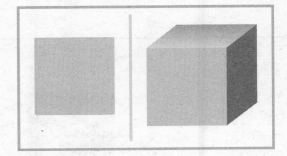  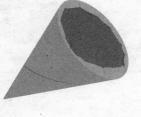

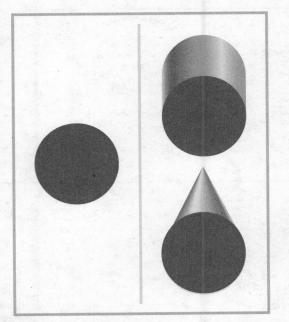    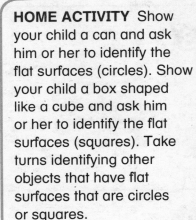

SOUP

Directions Say: *A cube has square flat surfaces. Draw a circle around the objects that have a square flat surface.* Have students look at the cylinder and cone in the box, identify the shape of their flat surfaces, and then mark an X on the objects that have a flat surface with that shape.

2

3

4

5

Topic 13 | Lesson 3

Name _____

Another Look!

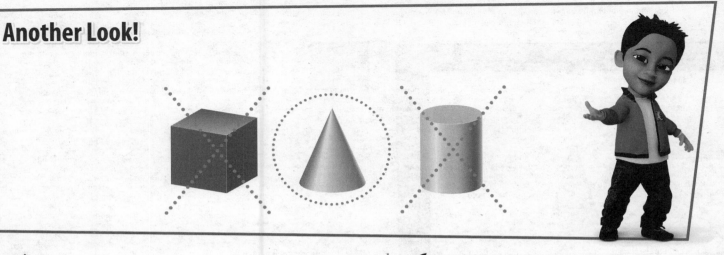

HOME ACTIVITY Pick an object in the room that is a cube, sphere, cone, or cylinder. Give your child clues about its shape, and ask him or her to guess which object you are thinking about. For example, a clue could be "Its flat surface is shaped like a square." (cube) Then invite your child to take a turn picking an object and giving you clues.

 1

 2

 3

 4

Directions Say: *Listen to the clues. After each clue, mark an X on any shape that does NOT fit the clue. I can roll. I do NOT have 2 flat surfaces. What shape am I? Draw a circle around the shape that fits all of the clues.* Read the clues to students. Have them mark an X on the shapes that do NOT fit the clues and draw a circle around the shape that the clues describe. Have students explain which clues helped them get the answer. **1** *I can roll. I CANNOT stack. What shape am I?* **2** *I can stack. I can slide. What shape am I?* **3** *I can roll. I have only 1 flat surface. What shape am I?* **4** *I can stack. I CANNOT roll. What shape am I?*

Directions Read the problem to students. Then have them use multiple problem-solving methods to solve the problem. Say: *Jackson is trying to solve a mystery. How are the shapes inside the frame similar? How can you find the answer?* 🖐 **Make Sense** *What shapes are outside of the frame? What shapes are inside the frame?* 🔟 **Be Precise** *What attribute do all of the shapes inside the frame have? Draw another shape like it inside the frame.* 🌲 **Use Tools** *Listen to the clues, and then draw 3 shapes inside the bottom frame that match the clues. I have 4 sides and 4 vertices. My sides are NOT the same length. What shape am I?*

Name _____

Another Look!

HOME ACTIVITY Give your child paper, pencil, and a small square shape, such as a square cracker or a square sticky-note. Ask him or her to draw another shape, such as a rectangle, using the square. Repeat with other shapes.

△ 9

Directions Say: *What shape is the pattern block? Use 6 pattern blocks to make a rectangle. Draw the new shape you made.* ★ *Have students use 9 pattern blocks to make a triangle, and then draw the new 2-D shape.*

2

3

4

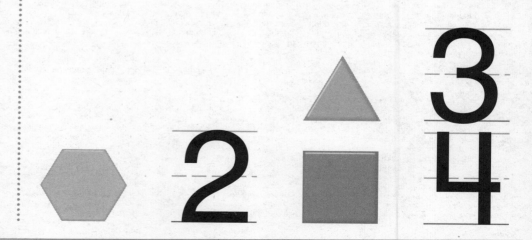

Directions **2** Have students use 5 pattern blocks to make a rectangle, and then draw the new 2-D shape. **3** Have students use pattern blocks to create a tree, and then draw it in the space. **4** **Higher Order Thinking** Have students use at least the pattern blocks shown to create a picture, and then draw it in the space.

Topic 13 | Lesson 5

Name _____

Additional Practice 13-6
Build 2-D Shapes

Another Look!

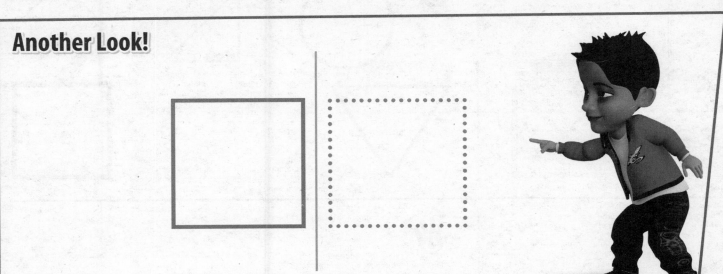

HOME ACTIVITY Take a look around your kitchen. With your child, look for materials that can be used to build different 2-D shapes. For example, your child can build shapes from dough, wooden spoons, or string.

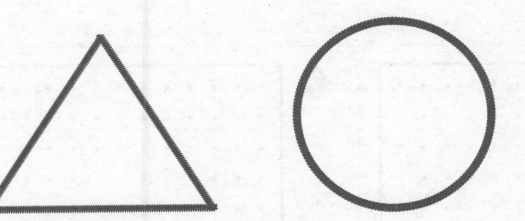

Directions Say: *This is a square. How do you know it is a square? Let's practice drawing a square.* Have students listen to the story:
★ Avery built shapes out of pipe cleaners. Mark an X on the triangle.

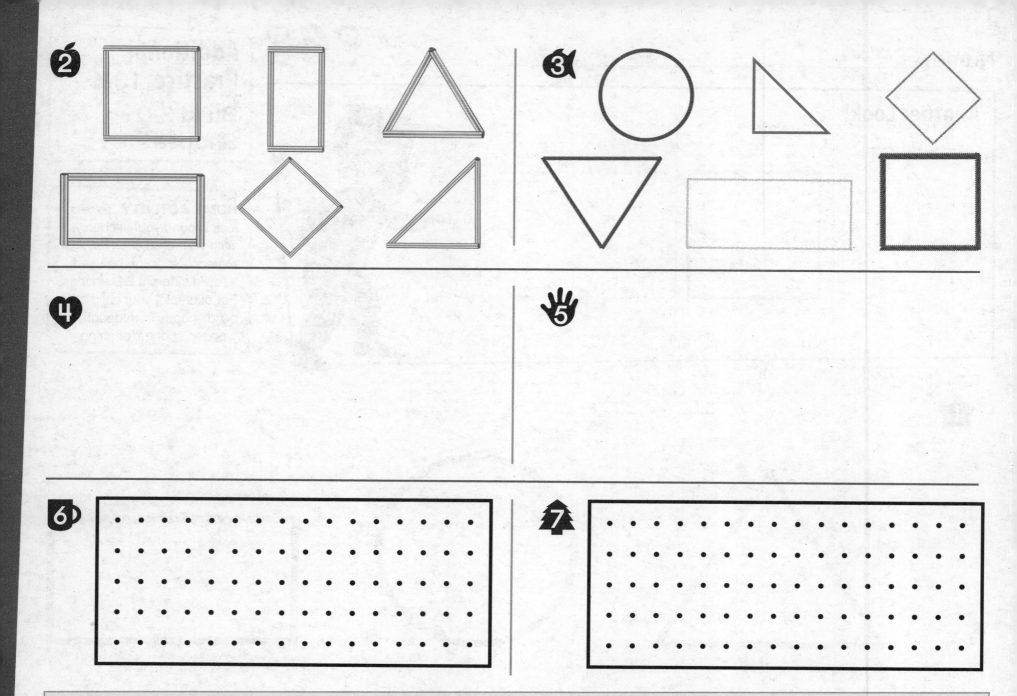

Directions Have students listen to each story: ② *Diego built 6 shapes out of straws. Mark an X on the shapes that are NOT rectangles.* ③ *Destiny built 6 shapes out of pipe cleaners. Mark an X on the shapes that are NOT triangles.* Have students: ④ draw a circle; ⑤ draw a triangle. ⑥ **Higher Order Thinking** Have students draw a rectangle that is NOT a square. ⑦ **Higher Order Thinking** Have students draw a rectangle that is also a square.

Video   Tools   Games

Another Look!

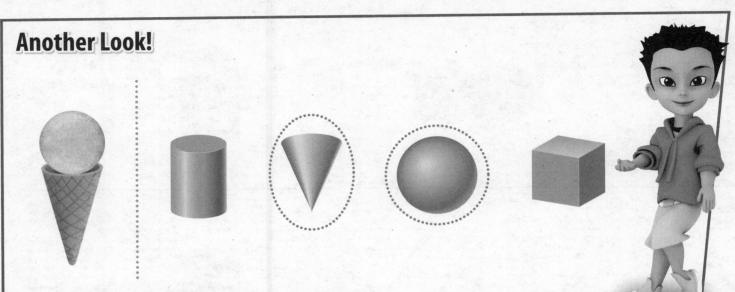

HOME ACTIVITY Have your child use materials from your house to build a 3-D shape.

⭐

🍎②

Directions Say: *Look at the object on the left. Draw a circle around the solid figures that make the shape.* Have students: ⭐ and ② draw a circle around the solid figures that build the shape.

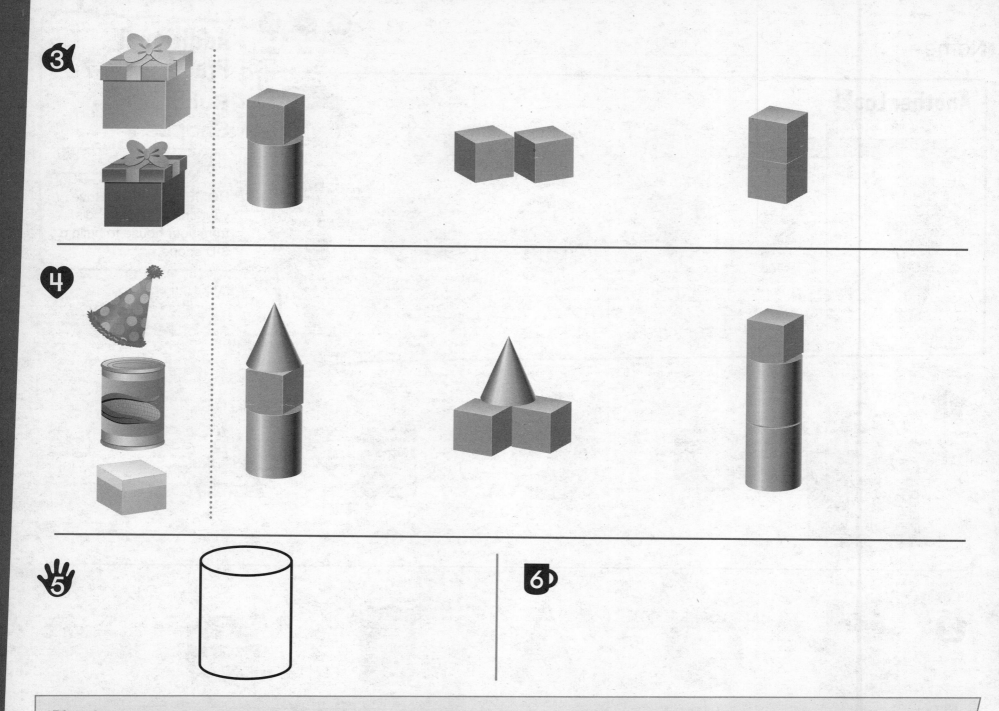

3

4

5

6

Name _____

Additional Practice 14-1

Describe and Compare by Length and Height

Another Look!

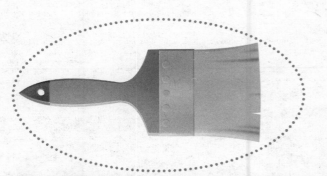

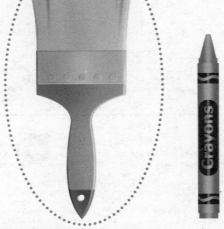

HOME ACTIVITY Set a kitchen spoon on a table. Ask your child to find 2 kitchen items that are longer than the spoon and 2 kitchen items that are shorter than the spoon. Then set a vase on the table. Ask your child to find 2 household objects that are taller than the vase and 2 household objects that are shorter than the vase.

 1

 2

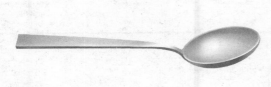

Directions Say: *Compare the objects on the left by length. Which object is longer? Draw a circle around the longer object. Now compare the objects by height. Draw a circle around the taller object. How are length and height related?* Have students: ⭐ mark an X on the shorter object or underline the objects if they are the same length; ② draw a circle around the taller object or underline the objects if they are the same height.

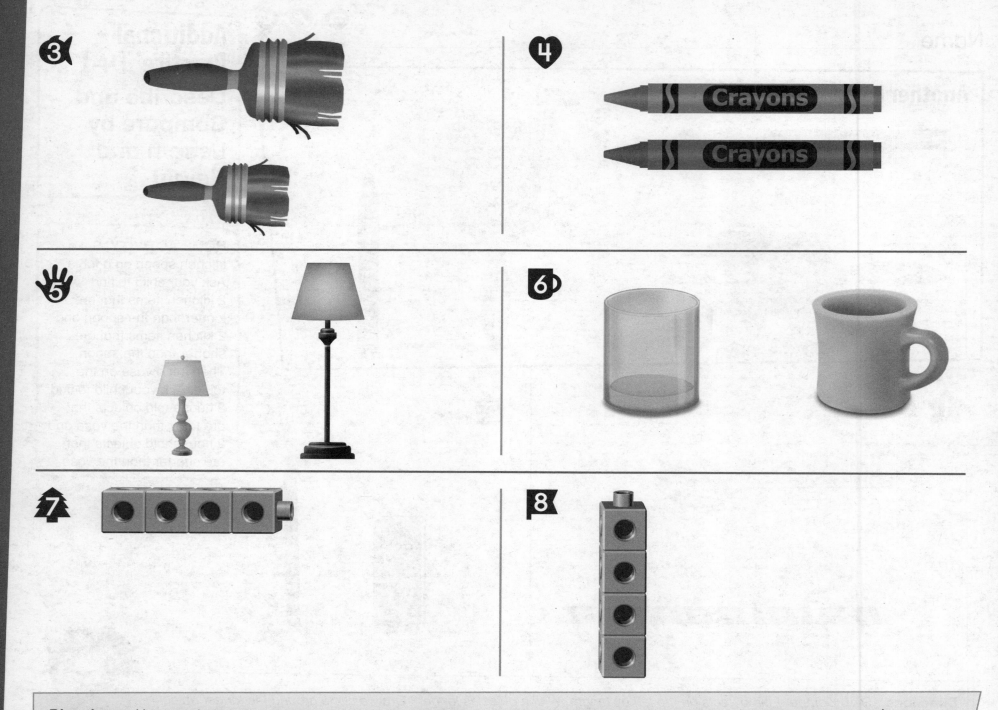

Name _____

Another Look!

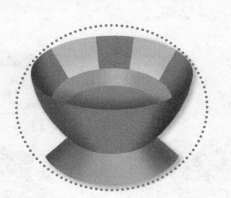

HOME ACTIVITY Set 2 pots that can hold different capacities on the table. Ask your child which one holds more and which one holds less. Check the answer by filling one pot with water and then pouring all or some of the water into the other pot. You can repeat using different containers.

Directions Say: *Which bowl holds more? How do you know? Draw a circle around it. Then mark an X on the bowl that holds less.* ⭐ Have students draw a circle around each container that holds more and mark an X on each container that holds less, or underline the containers if they hold the same amount.

4

Topic 14 | Lesson 2

Name _____

Another Look!

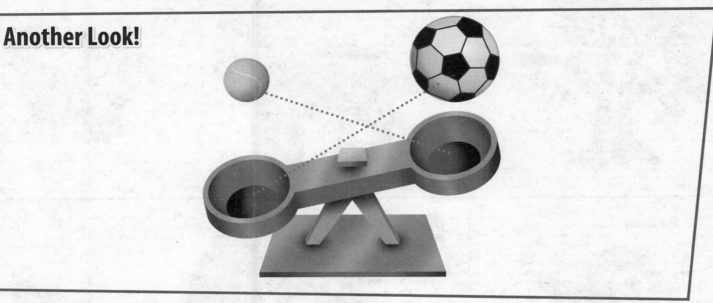

HOME ACTIVITY Ask your child to hold a slice of bread. Then ask your child to find something in your kitchen that is heavier than the slice of bread and then something that is lighter than the slice of bread.

★ 1

② 2

Directions Say: *Compare the objects. Which ball is heavier? Draw a line from the heavier ball to the lower side of the scale and a line from the lighter ball to the higher side of the scale.* ★ and ② Have students compare the objects, and then match the heavier object to the lower side of the scale and the lighter object to the higher side of the scale.

Directions ❸ **enVision® STEM** Have students draw a circle around the object that provides more shade, and then have them discuss what man-made objects protect them from the sun. ❹–❻ Have students draw a circle around the heavier object and mark an X on the lighter object. ❼ **Higher Order Thinking** Have students draw one object that is light and one object that is heavy. ❽ **Higher Order Thinking** Have students draw 2 objects that are the same weight.

 Topic 14 | **Lesson 3**

Name _____

Another Look!

HOME ACTIVITY Choose a few small objects, such as a cup, a book, and a spoon. Ask your child to describe each object, and then name tools that could be used to tell about different attributes of the object (e.g., balance scale, cube trains, measuring cup).

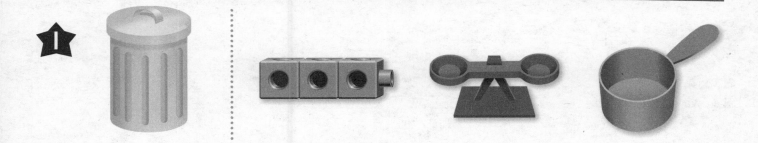

Directions Say: *Attributes, like how long something is, how heavy something is, or how much something holds, can be measured using tools. What attributes does a carton of milk have? Draw a circle around the tools that could be used to tell about these attributes.* ★ *and* ② *Have students look at the object on the left, identify the attributes that can be measured, and then draw a circle around the tools that could be used to tell about those attributes.*

3

4

5

6

Directions **3** and **4** Have students identify what attribute the tool on the left can measure, and then draw a circle around the object or objects that could be measured with that tool. **5 Higher Order Thinking** Have students identify the attribute that can be measured using the tool on the left, and then draw 2 objects that could be measured using that tool. **6 Higher Order Thinking** Have students draw an object that could be measured by the attributes of length, weight, and capacity.

 Topic 14 | Lesson 4

Name _____

Another Look!

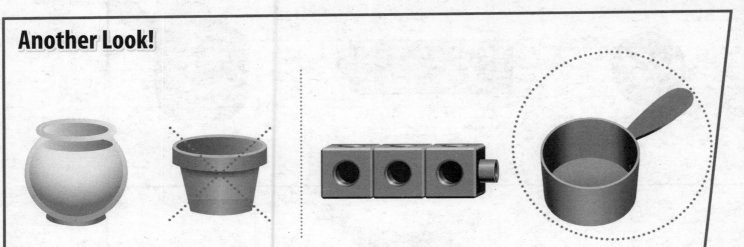

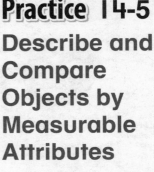

HOME ACTIVITY Show your child several household objects, such as a plate or a mug. Have him or her describe each object, and then name the tool(s) that could be used to tell about the different measurable attributes. Then have him or her compare two of the objects by one of the measurable attributes.

 ⭐

 ❷

Directions Say: *Attributes, like how tall something is, how heavy something is, or how much something holds, can be measured using tools. Look at the two objects. Draw an X on the object that holds less. Then circle the tool you can use to tell about how much an object holds.* ⭐ and ❷ Have students look at the object on the left and compare it with the object on the right. Then have them draw an X on the object that is lighter, or underline both objects if they are the same weight. Then have students draw a circle around the tool they can use to tell about the weights of the objects.

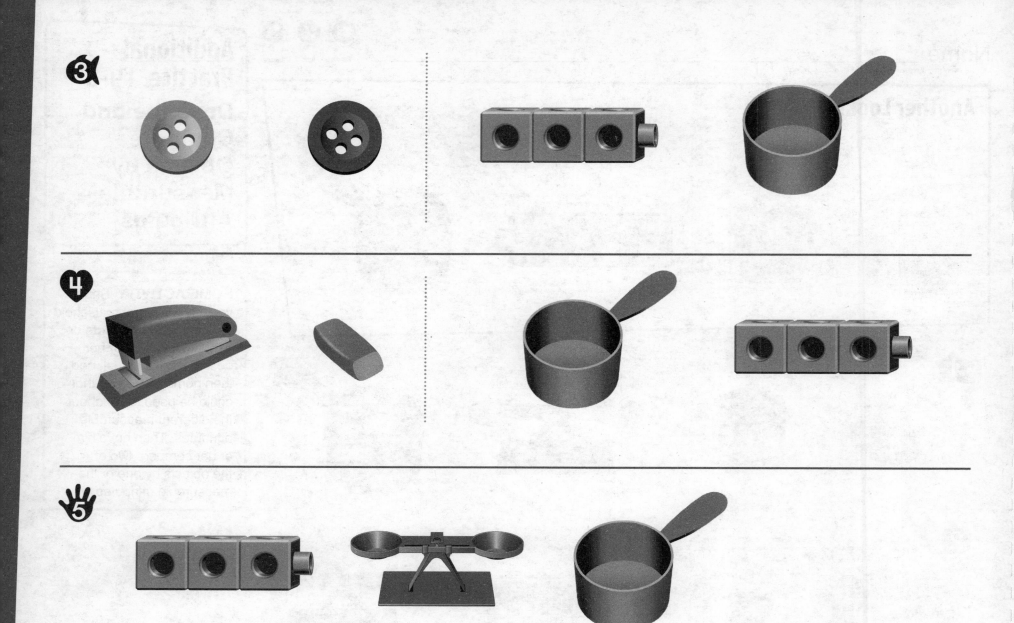

3

4

5

Directions **3** and **4** Have students look at the object on the left and compare it with the object on the right. Have them mark with an X the object that is shorter, or draw a line under each object if they are the same length. Then have students draw a circle around the tool that can be used to tell about the lengths of the objects. **5** **Higher Order Thinking** Have students draw an object. Then have them draw a circle around all the tools that can be used to measure attributes of the object.